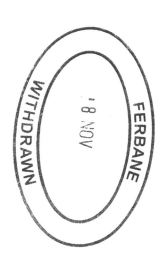

Boys Get Anorexia Too

Coping with male eating disorders in the family

Jenny Langley

P·C·P
Paul Chapman
Publishing

Paul Chapman Publishing
A SAGE Publications Company
1 Oliver's Yard
55 City Road
London EC1Y 1SP

SAGE Publications Inc.
2455 Teller Road
Thousand Oaks, California 91320

SAGE Publications India Pvt Ltd.
B-42, Panchsheel Enclave
Post Box 4109
New Delhi 110 017

Commissioning Editor: Barbara Maines
Editorial Team: Mel Maines, Wendy Ogden, Sarah Lynch
Designer: Nick Shearn

A catalogue record for this book is available from the British Library

Library of Congress Control Number 2005907004

ISBN10 1-4129-2021 3
ISBN13 978-1-4129 2021-6
ISBN10 1-4129-2022-1 (pbk)
ISBN13 978-1-4129-2022-3

Printed on paper from sustainable resources.

Printed in Great Britain by The Cromwell Press Ltd., Trowbridge, Wiltshire.

Contents

Foreword   v

Author's Note   vii

Preface   ix

Part One : About Anorexia in Boys   1

  1.   What is anorexia and what are the effects?   2

  2.   Boys don't get anorexia, do they?   4

  3.   Triggers for boy anorexia   5

  4.   What to look out for   8

  5.   Living with an anorexic boy   10

  6.   Effects on the family   22

  7.   Self-help   27

  8.   Treatment options   31

  9.   Therapy, therapy, therapy   43

  10. Healthy eating   49

  11. Caring for the carer   56

  12. Returning to normal life   61

  13. Do boys get other eating disorders?   65

Suggested Reading List   71

List of Useful Organisations   74

Part Two : Joe's Story   75

  14. Setting the scene – happy chaos   76

  15. Decline and fall   82

  16. The diagnosis – watch out for Rex   97

  17. The treatment – heaven or hell?   107

  18. Recovering too quickly? Watch out for Rex   131

  19. Coming home – will Rex come too?   165

  20. Moving on – Rex has gone!   172

Foreword

'Boys don't get anorexia' is a phrase that any parent who is concerned about a son who is losing too much weight or exercising excessively will hear at some time or other, hopefully from an uninformed friend or relative rather than a health professional.

Well boys DO get eating disorders and in this very personal and insightful book Jenny Langley looks at what it means to have a son who does in fact have anorexia.

Research, as well as anecdotal evidence, indicates that as many as 20 to 25% of school age adolescents who are affected by an eating disorder are male. However, the number of males diagnosed and seeking treatment is roughly half that. At Eating Disorders Association we know from callers to both our adult and youth helplines that males can find it hard to believe that they may have an eating disorder. Getting it diagnosed may be a struggle and finding appropriate treatment can be very problematic.

It is reassuring that with the approval of her son, Jenny has decided to write about the development of anorexia in boys and has taken the trouble to investigate and write about the wider issues in a way that will be helpful to parents and carers who are concerned about a young boy.

Any parent with an eating disorder in the family will know at first hand the problems that a young boy already caught up in the maelstrom of adolescence can both experience, and cause when anorexia arrives. Jenny writes about the way in which the disorder crept up on her family and then seemed to take over the household. Many parents will be relieved to know that they are not the only ones to experience this powerful and generally negative mix of emotions that surrounds and engulfs everyone nearby. Recent research indicates that boys affected by eating disorders are much more likely to blame themselves for their problems than girls do, complicating the already difficult process of recovery.

Jenny was lucky that the team involved with Joe's treatment involved her at every stage of the therapy. Although Jenny and the team often had very different views on Joe's progress, and at times the relationship was very strained, she and her family were never totally excluded. Many parents have found that talking to their doctor and even psychologists and psychiatrists is often not straightforward and many health professionals who struggle with these most complex of disorders hide behind a smokescreen of 'confidentiality' adding to parents' confusion and concern. Open communication and talking therapy is the key to recovery from eating disorders and except for those few cases where some form of abuse is at the heart of the problem, parents should be informed and involved with the whole treatment process.

Nevertheless, it is important to differentiate between the confidentiality of the consulting room and straightforward information about the progress of treatment. The relationship between patient and therapist can be slow to develop and difficult to unravel so it is entirely appropriate for the conversations during therapy to be confidential in every sense of the word. However, being prepared to discuss whether therapy is going as well as expected or is proving more difficult without needing to go into detail is the sort of information that should routinely be shared with parents or carers.

Many people find that pressured and confused health professionals can use the age of a patient (the NHS recognises 16 years old as an appropriate age for people to be treated as adults) to choose not to communicate with parents and carers who nevertheless are expected to care for the sufferer when they come home, either at weekends or at the end of the therapy. The Government Mental Health National Service Framework clearly states that patients must have a care plan that is drawn up with the involvement of the carer and the National Institute of Clinical Excellence (NICE) guidelines specifically recommend that all family members should be included in the treatment of children and adolescents with eating disorders.

Sadly, many carers find themselves having to fight to be included in the therapeutic process instead of being there by invitation from the professionals. This leads to even greater stress and disharmony in the family. Many parents and carers will find the practical tips Jenny provides on how best to approach medical professionals initially, and how to stay involved as treatment progresses, very useful.

As many parents have discovered, the problems do not disappear when the hospital takes over and the slow painful climb of Jenny's son back to recovery is recounted in uncomfortable detail. Ultimately however this is a story of hope. Joe does recover eventually and although life is by no means the same as before, it does return to a new normality.

Steve Bloomfield
Head of Communications
Eating Disorders Association

Author's Note

It is common knowledge that eating disorders, and in particular anorexia, are a girl thing, and we have all read articles containing startling facts such as:

> One in 20 women will suffer from an eating disorder in their lifetime.
> In Britain, anorexia and bulimia have reached catastrophic levels.
> Maureen Rice, Observer Sunday July 29, 2001

Of course it is also logical to assume that men and boys are not totally immune, but how many incidences of male eating disorders have you heard of? Certainly up until my son was afflicted I hadn't ever heard of any examples. It turned out neither had my GP, any of the teachers at my son's school, nor any of my friends or work colleagues. So it was a huge shock when my 12-year-old son started to disappear before my eyes. He was a gifted child, in the streamed class at school, and a great sportsman representing the school at football, his main passion, as well as cross-country, athletics, rugby, cricket and swimming, and he was very popular with his peers at school. His anorexia developed startlingly quickly, he lost 25% of his body weight in four months, before collapsing and being rushed into hospital. Six months on and after three and a half months in a residential adolescent unit, I am pleased to say that he was well on the way to recovery. Two years further on and he is a thriving, healthy and happy 15-year-old, who is probably stronger both mentally and physically, having beaten his illness. The relapse rate is high for anorexics, but we are keeping our fingers crossed that this won't happen to us, and we are looking forward to him having a healthy and happy future.

The reason for writing this book, in which I describe our experiences and outline the treatment options available, is that we felt totally alone as parents of an anorexic boy. The eating disorder societies were very helpful and sympathetic but could not put me in contact with other families who had experienced boy anorexia. The professionals assured me that boy anorexia is not unheard of, and especially in the younger age group the balance between boys and girls is more even, but as far as I know there is no literature on this specific subject. I managed to locate a couple of American books on male eating disorders, which have been written in the last couple of years. They were very interesting, and at least acknowledged that there has been an explosion in the incidence of eating disorders in the male population over the last few decades. This provided me with some comfort, but didn't really provide me with any guidance as to the best course of action, being a mother in the UK, watching her son starve himself almost to death in front of her eyes. I would like to think that this book will give hope and practical guidance to any family going through a similar experience.

Anorexia is a terrifying experience for any family to go through, but remember:

- Boys can get anorexia too.
- Anorexia can be beaten.
- Look forward not back.
- Never give up hope.

And most importantly, you are not alone.

Preface

Tuesday 12 March 2002

Joe started moving around his room at 5.30 am. Since his weight had dropped below 36 kg I knew he hadn't been sleeping very well. I am a light sleeper myself and was on a high state of alert to any sounds in the night from my eldest son. His weight had dropped from 42 kg to 32 kg in just four months, and he was in a constant state of agitation and anxiety. We were still awaiting the results from endless blood tests, and had yet to rule out a seemingly endless list of terrible diseases that could be the root cause. I had lain awake night after night considering illnesses ranging from leukemia, and stomach cancer, to thyroid problems, and glandular fever. But in my heart of hearts I knew my son was suffering from an acute case of anorexia, and as every day passed it was taking a firmer grip.

At 6.30 am, after an hour of intense repetitive exercise (mainly press-ups and sit-ups) in his bedroom, Joe went downstairs. He liked to have breakfast on his own, as he had become extremely self-conscious about eating in front of other people, even within our family. I knew that if I tried to force him to eat with us, or even to suggest he should eat a little more, he would become deeply upset and eat nothing.

Getting from his bedroom to the kitchen involved a whole array of rituals. Joe had become deeply superstitious and believed that some terrible fate would overcome him if he did not do each and every one of his rituals, which seemed to be increasing as each day passed. First Joe stopped at the boundary between his bedroom and the hall. He stared, for a few seconds, at the metal strip separating the two carpets, and then carefully stepped over it, as if stepping on it might cause an explosion. Each step on the staircase was like an individual challenge, with Joe placing first his right foot quickly followed by his left foot on each individual step. Halfway down the stairs Joe did fifty to sixty pull-ups as he could reach up to the banister on the landing above. He then did another set of pull-ups when he walked past the stairs in the hallway on the way to the kitchen. Once in the kitchen Joe would touch all the surfaces on the way to the fridge. Breakfast for Joe used to be one or two large bowls of cereal, but now it was the same everyday, a Muller Light yoghurt. I had tried filling the fridge with high fat yoghurts, but then Joe would have no breakfast at all. As for all his meals, Joe ate a little less each day.

At this stage he ate about two thirds of the yoghurt, and on a good day might have a quarter glass of squash or water.

After breakfast Joe did twenty minutes of sit-ups in front of the TV, and then sat on the edge of the sofa, alternately tapping his feet on the floor and counting on his fingers. By 8 am, Joe looked exhausted, his skin had a grey pallor and his eyes and cheeks were sunken hollows.

My friend Sophie was doing the school run that morning. I watched as Joe shuffled out to the car and slumped into the back seat to continue counting on his fingers and tapping his feet for the ten minute journey to school. Sophie rang me as soon as she got home. We had discussed Joe's deterioration several times already that week, but she was particularly alarmed at how ill Joe looked that morning. He had staggered from the car, clutching his briefcase as if it were a dead weight, and Sophie had been very tempted to scoop him up and bring him straight home. However, I knew that the school would call me immediately if Joe wasn't coping in class, and we had stopped him doing any sport a week before because of his fragile condition.

I tried to focus on my work for the next few hours, but there were no real stories in the stock market and it was a struggle to get the clients interested in anything. The morning dragged and every time my home phone rang I leapt out of my skin, thinking that Joe had perhaps collapsed at school. But he coped quite well that particular morning and even managed a smile when I picked him up at lunchtime. He had been coming home for lunch for several weeks now because he couldn't eat the school lunches in front of his school friends. He had the same thing for lunch everyday: a ham sandwich, a banana and a chocolate bar with a small drink. This doesn't sound too bad, but each day he would eat slightly less. Today he managed about half the sandwich, a bite of the banana and the chocolate bar and half a glass of orange squash. After lunch Joe felt really bloated so he did half an hour of sit-ups and press-ups before I took him back to school for a couple of lessons. I knew that if I tried to stop Joe, he would either burst into tears or get extremely angry, both of which were distressing for both of us, so I said nothing.

I picked Joe up again from school at 3 pm, two hours earlier than normal because Joe was no longer able to join in with any sporting activities. About a week earlier he had collapsed into a heap of tears after a rugby session, because he was so exhausted, and everyone agreed it was probably best if Joe stopped doing games until he was a little stronger. He asked if we could go for a walk in the local Country Park. We did this often, as Joe seemed to find this calmed him down. He couldn't walk very far and we walked slowly, with Joe dragging his left foot along the ground as though he was somehow crippled, but this was just another of the habits he had developed. As we walked through the park Joe made a point of picking up even the smallest pieces of litter and making a detour to the nearest bin. When he had first started doing this I had thought it was a very good habit, but like all his habits it had become a complete obsession. On this particular day Joe talked quite openly about his illness. "Mummy I wish I could get better, but it hurts so much when I eat too much. I know I need to put on weight but I'm scared of getting fat. Do you think the doctors can help? I really want to get better for the football season because I could be captain of the first team at school." I gave Joe all the reassurance that I could, but I was petrified over what the future would bring. Joe had declined so quickly and whilst we were having a sensible conversation walking in the park, I knew that as soon as we got home and the issue of dinner was raised, there would be another battle, as the anorexia reared its ugly head and distorted my young son's brain. Given that Joe seemed happy to talk I asked him why he thought he had become ill, and was surprised to get a fairly detailed answer. "Mummy I have just become obsessed about losing weight and I don't know how to stop. I thought if I lost some weight I would be able to play football better, and I wanted to win the school cross-country run. Now I can't even play football, and I know I won't be able to compete in the school cross-country next week. Also a boy last term said I had a big bum. I know he didn't mean any harm, but it really upset me, and I can't cope with being in the streamed class anymore, it's just too hard." By this stage Joe was sobbing, we stopped walking and I put my arms around his fragile frame. I hoped and prayed that this was a turning point. Joe now acknowledged his illness, we had a huge mountain to climb to restore Joe to health, but at least Joe was willing to try, and that was the first big hurdle to get over. By this stage we had been walking, albeit very slowly, for twenty minutes. Joe was exhausted so we returned to the car and headed home.

Once Joe was settled in front of the TV, I phoned his form teacher. Peter had been brilliant from the very first day that I had alerted him to my concerns over Joe's weight, and by this stage we spoke every day. He told me that Joe had had an uneventful day at school, but all the teachers were worried about him and Joe was a constant topic of conversation in the staff room. Peter was concerned that Joe was becoming more and more withdrawn socially. Once a popular boy with his classmates, he was now sitting on his own in class and rather than joining in with the games at break, he was standing away from the crowd, watching the antics going on but not wanting to be involved. A few of Joe's closest friends had tried to bring him back within the group, but with little effect, and I knew from my conversations with their mums that the boys couldn't understand what had happened to the Joe that they knew so well. Peter also mentioned that Joe's writing had become even more flowery in the past week, almost to the extent of being totally illegible. Peter had alerted me to this a couple of weeks earlier and it was another tangible indicator that Joe was declining as every week went by. Peter and I agreed that Joe would not be able to attend school full time for much longer, but Peter was happy for Joe to attend on a part-time basis, even if only for half an hour at a time. I relayed my conversation with Joe in the park to Peter and he agreed that this was a major step forward, and said he would of course do anything he could to help.

I picked up Joe's younger brother Tom at 5.15 pm. Joe came with me and sat huddled like a little old man in the car, chewing his knuckles. Joe's hands had become scaly and raw in recent weeks, as he chewed nervously on them much of the time. Tom was in his normal happy mood, and chattered away about his day at school as we drove home. But once we got home Tom was careful to keep out of Joe's way. They had become quite distant in recent weeks. Tom couldn't understand what had happened to his big brother and didn't really want to talk about it. His way of coping was to keep busy doing things which didn't involve Joe, and he spent as much time as possible out of the house playing with his friends from the neighbouring houses.

I prepared a simple dinner for the boys: fish fingers, pasta, peas and carrots. Tom demolished his plateful in record time and disappeared outside to play on the trampoline. Joe was a different story, he pushed his food around the plate, and after twenty minutes had managed one fish finger, six pieces of pasta and a couple of mouthfuls of peas and carrots. He then purposefully placed his knife and fork neatly together on the plate and glared at me, daring me to say something. I gently tried to persuade him to have just a few more mouthfuls, but he couldn't. He clutched his stomach, which was rock hard from all the sit-ups and malnutrition, and was obviously in considerable pain. I backed off, exhausted from this daily battle. We desperately needed professional medical help. I had finally managed to get an appointment with a child psychiatrist which was now just two days away, so I had decided that the best policy between now and then was to keep Joe as calm as possible, and hope that he didn't lose too much more weight.

On the dot of 7 pm, after half an hour of sit-ups and press-ups, Joe went upstairs for his daily shower, doing his pull-ups on the stairs as normal. I followed him up and got him to step on the scales. 32 kg, another kilo lost in the past week. Joe was secretly delighted. I was devastated. I left him to his shower, which always took half an hour. He washed his hands meticulously throughout the day and scrubbed his body thoroughly every evening. He left the bathroom spotless with the towel hanging perfectly on the rail. Then he retreated to his immaculately tidy bedroom to read his Dorling Kindersley children's bible. This was another of his comforts, he read out loud, tracing the words with his finger.

At 8.30 pm I went up to say goodnight. Joe looked utterly exhausted, his shrivelled body totally swamped by pyjamas that had fit him perfectly well just four months earlier. He hugged me for a long time, I felt I was losing him to this terrible disease and he sensed my anxiety. "Don't worry Mummy, I'll be OK. Please don't be upset, it makes me feel really bad." I retreated back downstairs and prepared supper for my husband James. James could sense that we had had another bad day, but simply didn't know what else to say. As we sat down for supper we could hear a rhythmic thudding coming through the ceiling from Joe's bedroom, yet more sit-ups or press-ups, just in case he had eaten too much for supper and might put a gram or two weight back on. I burst into floods of tears and James came around the table to give me a big reassuring hug. I kept repeating, "I just want my son back," but there was no way of knowing when, or if, this would ever happen.

Part One

About Anorexia in Boys

1. What is anorexia and what are the effects?

Anorexia nervosa is the best known of a range of illnesses classified as eating disorders. Anorexia nervosa literally means 'loss of appetite for nervous reasons'. The main diagnostic criteria for anorexia is that there is a weight loss leading to a body weight of at least 15% below the normal weight for height or age, although anorexia itself is much more complex than just loss of appetite or weight loss. Those with anorexia will deliberately starve themselves until they are very ill, and in a small number of cases until they die. Anorexics are terrified of gaining weight and if they feel they have eaten even a tiny morsel too much they will exercise obsessively to get rid of the calories. They are often obsessed with the amount of calories in each type of food. They will often encourage those around them to eat more, whilst continually cutting back on their food intake. Anorexics desperately want to be in control, and the one thing they feel they can control is their food intake. Sadly they soon find that they have lost control and that their anorexia is controlling every aspect of their lives. When he was well on his way to recovery Joe said to me, "Mummy, I just wanted to lose a bit of weight for my sport and it just got completely out of control."

But anorexia is much more than just being about food. The sufferer is normally deeply unhappy about some aspect of his life and will have a very low self-esteem. Many sufferers feel that their illness gives them the attention from their loved ones that perhaps they felt they weren't getting before. Finding out what has made the sufferer unhappy or craving attention can be very difficult and sometimes impossible to work out. There are literally hundreds of reasons why young people suffer from anorexia nervosa. The most important thing to remember is to look forward, not back. Often the cause is irrelevant to the recovery and most anorexics do eventually recover.

What are the effects of self-starvation? A period of sustained weight loss and malnutrition will result in the patient suffering from many symptoms, and damage can be severe. There are many symptoms of anorexia and not every patient suffers from all of them. I mention some of the more common symptoms below and you will find that the more you read, the more symptoms you will discover. It may well be worth alerting your son as to what could happen to his body if he continues to lose weight and be malnourished over a long period of time.

The short-term effects of anorexia are usually apparent fairly early on. In girls, as well as periods stopping, their ovaries and uterus may start to shrink, and growth in general stops. In boys you don't have such a clear indicator as loss of periods, but ongoing puberty may be arrested or slowed down, and your son may revert to a more childlike state. This is certainly what happened with Joe. As he lost weight he looked younger, he spoke more quietly and became much less physically active. Many anorexics quickly become depressed, may suffer from poor concentration and lose powers of memory. They may also become irrational and unreasonable as a result of subtle changes to the balance of chemicals within the body, and most will suffer from a feeling of low self-esteem. Some develop an unsightly fine downy hair on their back and face called lanugo. It is one of the body's ways of keeping warm. Muscles may become weak after a period of malnutrition and major nerves can become prone to pressure damage. The heart starts to pump less efficiently and this often leads to an abnormally low pulse rate and blood pressure. This in turn causes dizzy spells and the sufferer constantly feels cold and tired. A poor diet may also lead to anaemia, which also causes tiredness and the sufferer becomes very pale. A poor diet may also lead to constipation, a feeling of bloatedness, and stomach pains, which can be severe. Joe had episodes when he lay curled up on the ground screaming in agony, having eaten just a few morsels of food. All of these effects reverse quite quickly once normal eating patterns are resolved.

The long-term effects of anorexia are not so obvious, but can be of greater concern. In girls long-term loss of periods can lead to infertility, and the abnormally low hormone levels can lead to osteoporosis, resulting in bones that are weak and can fracture very easily. Other hormones such as thyroid and growth hormones can also be affected by long-term starvation. The reduced hormone levels have similar effects in boys in terms of infertility, bone density, growth etc. Internal organs are inevitably affected by a lengthy period of starvation, and in particular the heart and kidneys may suffer irreversible damage. Circulation of blood around the body can also be dramatically restricted, following a lengthy period of malnutrition, and in severe cases this can lead to tissue death in the extremities. Many long-term anorexics have suffered from gangrene and some have needed below the knee amputations. Unfortunately some anorexics die but thankfully the percentage is quite low. Some can no longer cope with their illness and take their own life, others die from organ failure, but I must stress these are very extreme cases. Many anorexics recover and live perfectly normal lives. Many learn to live with their anorexia.

2. Boys don't get anorexia, do they?

Anorexia is certainly more common in girls and one of the symptoms that GP's tend to look for, as an indicator of anorexia, is loss of periods. There is no such obvious indicator for boys. One of the main problems in recognising anorexia in boys is that lots of teenage boys go through stretch and grow phases in which they become extremely skinny despite still having a healthy appetite. Many boys are naturally very skinny even before entering puberty, but are in excellent health. When Joe first lost weight we thought he was simply going through a normal teenage stretch and grow phase, and my younger son is going through a very similar growth phase now that he is twelve. The big difference with Joe was that he didn't stop losing weight, he gradually ate less and less, he became very pale and was always cold, he became tearful and depressed, he became distant from his friends and much more clingy to me. This was a boy who had previously been full of vitality and energy, very popular with his peers, very sporty, in the top stream at school and had a very healthy appetite. As his character started to change I thought that maybe he was just going through a difficult phase of puberty, but then his behaviour became quite extreme. Before his anorexia was finally diagnosed he was subjected to every medical examination you can imagine. I lay awake at night worrying that he had leukemia, some sort of other blood disorder or cancer. When he became fearful of fluids I worried he had rabies. He physically disappeared and mentally he had become a stranger, withdrawing from normal life before our very eyes. It was as if someone else had possessed him. We called this person Rex.

The fact is boys do get anorexia and other eating disorders. Since Joe's illness I have come across several other cases similar to ours, and many parents have asked me for advice having noticed that their son's eating habits and/or personality has taken a turn for the worse. Most commentators on eating disorders will tell you that about 10% of sufferers are male but it is almost impossible to work out how this figure has been arrived at. In the younger age group (early teens) a higher proportion are boys, but figures vary enormously depending on which study has been used. Joe's psychiatrist told me that in his current practice he had treated nine patients with very severe anorexia that required in-patient treatment. Three of those were boys! What is clear is that eating disorders in young people are on the increase and this includes boys as well as girls.

3.   Triggers for boy anorexia

Many of my friends have asked me, 'Did you ever find out what caused Joe's anorexia?' The straightforward answer is no. However we have a few ideas about what could have been contributing factors:

- He went through a very early puberty. It is no coincidence that many cases of anorexia start in puberty, both in boys and girls. With girls the reason seems more obvious as they look in the mirror and see a more rounded shape developing. Boys tend to be happier with their developing a more muscular physique, but if a boy has a very early puberty he might not appreciate the changes that are happening to his body and making him different from his peers. In addition, the raging hormones can trigger irrational behaviour in either sex.

- Joe was, and having recovered from his illness is still, a very talented sportsman. This is his explanation. "I thought I would be an even better sportsman if I lost a little weight. I felt really good when I lost weight and to start with all my friends commented on how good I looked. The trouble was it got out of control and I found I couldn't stop losing weight. I just got scared of eating in case I put weight back on." There are numerous cases of sportsmen restricting their diet for their sport and developing an eating disorder. Consider jockeys, gymnasts, light weight boxers, long distance runners, cyclists and ballet dancers who can all justify restricting their diet to ensure they maintain an 'optimum' weight for their sport.

- Joe is the eldest child of a complex family. He has one sibling, three half siblings and three stepsiblings. It is likely that he felt he was always the last in the pecking order of all these younger children. For years he may have been craving more of our attention without us realising. He always seemed such a happy boy with a healthy appetite, and one who loved his sport. When I read *The Best Little Girl in the World* by Steven Levenkron, it made me realise how an outwardly happy and well-balanced child could actually be feeling very lonely and left out by the demands of other children within the family.

- Research has shown that pre-term babies are more likely to suffer from behavioural difficulties including eating disorders. Joe was born six weeks prematurely so this could have been a contributory factor.

There could have been many other triggers of Joe's anorexia, but he didn't bring them to our attention. Of course we agonised about such things as our family structure, was he being overstretched at school, was he being bullied? It is important to note that anorexia can appear in any family setting and in any social situation. We are a large complex family but many small nuclear families, that appear to have no problems, have been affected by a visit from anorexia. Children from all walks of life are vulnerable. Some typical triggers might include:

- An overweight child being teased or bullied at school. Comments might be made in jest and in a friendly manner, but then taken to heart.

- A highly academic child might be bullied by less able children and see food as a way to control his life.

- A less academic child might see weight loss as the only thing he can achieve positive results with.

- A child whose parents are constantly dieting might follow suit.

- A child who has seen an overweight parent or relative suffer a heart attack might seek to prevent this happening to him by cutting back on food.

- Abuse within the family often leads to an eating disorder.

- An overprotective or over dominant mother has often been blamed in the past for her child's eating disorder.

- A passive or absent father has also been often cited as a reason for a child developing eating problems.

Social pressures might cause a child to start dieting and exercising. Within our culture young men who have a slim and athletic build are portrayed as being popular, attractive, healthy and successful in life. A young boy with puppy fat might feel he has to take drastic measures to achieve this image as soon as possible.

As well as these social triggers, eating disorders can also be triggered by chemical or biological factors. Chemical imbalances in the brain can lead to all sorts of behavioural disorders. It is also increasingly believed that there may be a genetic link, and certainly eating disorders seem to run in families.

The bottom line is that every case is different. No one type of person gets an eating disorder, and no two people with an eating disorder are exactly alike. The common features seem to be that people who develop eating disorders suffer from a very low self-esteem, and many find it difficult to express their true feelings or explain what is making them unhappy.

Of course we will never really know exactly what triggered Joe's illness, and like most parents of anorexic children we went through many months of agonising over what we could have done better to prevent our son almost starving himself to death. Joe's key worker made me feel much better when she made two points in our first meeting:

1. It is much more important to look forward, not back. What caused Joe's illness may well be totally irrelevant to his recovery and his future. Of course if we discovered, during the course of his therapy, that there was something in his life that was making him unhappy then we could endeavour to change it. In many cases of anorexia the initial triggers remain a complete mystery.

2. All families are dysfunctional in some way. However simple or complex your family set-up, there are always disagreements and periods where some members are less happy than others are. Of course we should examine our family set-up, and try to change if necessary, but we shouldn't assume that there must be something terribly wrong with our family simply because our son had developed anorexia. Family therapy (more of this later) is a very good forum for examining the family set-up and discussing if any changes might be beneficial.

4. What to look out for

Anorexic boys and girls display similar physical and psychological changes as their illness starts to take hold, although boys are more likely to be concerned with their athleticism, whilst girls are much more concerned with their basic body image.

As I have already mentioned, one of the key difficulties in diagnosing anorexia in boys is that lots of boys go through extremely skinny phases whilst maintaining a healthy appetite. If you suspect that your son is suffering from an eating disorder, it is an invaluable exercise to note down any changes to his behaviour however small they might seem at the time. As the weeks go past you may well forget that he didn't used to have some of these funny habits. Another key difficulty is that many of the changes in behaviour could easily be caused by the onset of puberty. However, as the list starts to grow you will soon sense that something else is having a profound effect on your son.

These are some of the things to look out for:

- Has your son lost weight or failed to gain weight for some time?
- Is your son exercising more than he used to?
- Have you noticed that he is eating less?
- Can you find out if he is eating less at school?
- Have you noticed your son excluding certain types of food?
- Is your son playing with his food or cutting it up into tiny pieces?
- Has your son developed any other rituals around eating?
- Does your son comment on other people's shapes and sizes?
- Does your son encourage those around him to eat, whilst eating very little himself?
- Has your son suddenly become more attentive to his personal hygiene?
- Has your son suddenly become much more neat and tidy?
- Has your son become more concerned about his schoolwork and/or his position in class?
- Has your son started wearing bigger and baggier clothes or asking for you to buy them?

- Have you noticed your son doing repetitive exercises at home?

- Has your son developed any other repetitive habits?

- Has your son changed his social circle?

- Has your son withdrawn from the family?

- Has your son developed a temper or is he displaying dramatic mood swings?

- Does he often seem sad and tearful?

- Have any aspects of his behaviour become irrational?

- Has he developed any superstitions?

- Have you noticed any change in his bathroom habits?

- Have you noticed any change in his sleep patterns?

- Does he get angry if you confront him about his weight and/or eating or exercise habits?

- Does your son look pale and does he complain of constantly being cold or tired?

- Is his skin unusually dry?

- Has he grown any fine downy hair (not like the increase in normal body hair during puberty)?

- Has anyone else in your family, at school or in your social circle commented on a change in his appearance and/or behaviour?

The list gives you an idea of the sorts of things to look out for. Different boys will show different changes in appearance and behaviour. Many of the above, when taken on their own, could be explained away as normal for a child going through puberty. The key is to look at all the changes together. Within two months of my becoming concerned about Joe's health, I could have answered yes to most of the questions listed above.

If you are concerned about your son's weight and/or diet it is worth looking out for some of these other changes in behaviour and **write them down.**

If you decide to seek professional help you are much more likely to be listened to if you can give a detailed account of how your son's behaviour has changed. (More on this in Treatment Options, Chapter 8.)

5.   Living with an anorexic boy

The Preface describes a day in the life of our son when anorexia had taken over his life. He was obsessed with rituals, he could only eat and drink tiny amounts, he could hardly walk up the stairs and he couldn't think straight. One day is bad enough but when it goes on day after day you start to think your life is never going to return to normal. Luckily my husband was extremely supportive, but I could see the effect it was having on my younger son. He was becoming more and more withdrawn and his schoolwork was suffering. His school knew about the problems at home but they couldn't do anything to improve his concentration at this difficult time.

As a family we felt incredibly isolated having an anorexic boy in our midst. Everyone knows about teenage girls getting anorexia, but don't understand that boys can suffer too. I scoured the Internet for books, but I couldn't find any literature on eating disorders in teenage boys. I found some American books about eating disorders in men, which were useful as background reading, but didn't give me any practical tips on how to cope with an anorexic boy. We felt guilty. Most families who experience anorexia feel guilty at some stage, but we felt extra guilty because our son had anorexia. We must have done something extra bad because: 'Boys don't get anorexia.'

Once we had got over the initial feelings of guilt we were able to focus all our energy on helping our son to get better. In this chapter I describe some of the common features that families face when anorexia comes to stay. Much of this chapter is drawn from our own personal experience, but I have also included some traits that anorexics often display, but that we didn't experience first hand.

Anorexic boys don't behave like normal boys. A prolonged period of starvation causes chemical changes in the brain, which can lead to dramatic changes in character and behaviour. Anorexic boys often develop strange habits and superstitious rituals. They become withdrawn from their friends and many become very clingy to their parents. As anorexia takes over they become irrational and have terrible mood swings and temper tantrums. Living with an anorexic boy is exhausting and can push the strongest family to breaking point. The more we read around the subject, the more we realised that Joe's behaviour was fairly typical of an anorexic teenager. Whilst it was still difficult to cope with, it made it easier to know that other families had faced similar challenges and survived. Of course, virtually everything we read described the behaviour patterns in girls, but as Joe's illness developed we came to realise that there are many similarities between behaviour traits in boys and girls. In our experience Joe was more ritualistic and obsessive than many of the girls we came across, but on the other hand he wasn't as secretive or manipulative either.

In this chapter, I describe Joe's anorexic behaviour and commonly occurring anorexic behaviour under the following headings:

- Food
- Exercise
- Rituals
- Weight
- Clothes
- Moods, tantrums and irrational behaviour.

Some of the habits and rituals might make you laugh; others might make you cringe. If your son is showing signs of developing anorexia, then this chapter should prepare you for the worst. It is better to be prepared and to face up to the effect that his behaviour might have on the rest of the family. Families that stick their heads in the sand and let their anorexic child do whatever he wants are soon likely to find that his anorexia is thriving and the whole family has been taken over by his anorexia.

Food

These are some of the rituals Joe developed. Some appeared at home when he was cutting down on food. Others appeared when he was on his re-feeding programme at the in-patient unit and he couldn't face eating the entire enormous meal placed in front of him.

- Avoiding certain food types – chocolate, chips, cheese, cream, full fat dairy products.
- Cutting out meals – Joe started by cutting out on his school lunch and snacks.
- Reducing the amount eaten each meal – for two months Joe ate slightly less at each meal at home.
- Cutting out fluids – Joe was slightly unusual in this respect. He found it difficult to swallow anything. It is more common for anorexics to drink lots of diet drinks and/or water to fill themselves up.
- Complaining of stomach pains – as Joe lost more and more weight his stomach pains became more and more severe.

- Encouraging other family members to eat more – Joe was forever giving extra snacks to his younger brother.

- Eating slowly – as Joe found it more and more difficult to eat, it took him longer to eat each tiny meal.

- Playing with food – this is a favourite anorexic trait. Food is chased around the plate, but never quite makes it into the mouth. Joe used to hope we wouldn't notice he hadn't eaten anything.

- Dropping food off the plate onto the table, onto someone else's plate, into the dog or onto the floor. We didn't have any pets, but very often one of us would find we suddenly had extra potatoes or meat on our plates.

- Eating incredibly quickly in order to get the ordeal over as quickly as possible. Once Joe had accepted his re-feeding plan, he started eating so rapidly that he couldn't possibly taste the food.

Other common food habits and rituals include:

- Eating piles of low calorie and/or high fibre food such as fruit, vegetables, salad and low fat yoghurts, but eating little else.

- Reducing the calories of food that is eaten. Anorexics have been known to water down milk, take nuts out of cereal, put a low calorie fruit bar in a Mars bar wrapper.

- Cutting food into tiny pieces and then only eating a few of them.

- Obsessions about the how food is positioned on the plate or how the table is set.

- Wanting to become vegetarian or vegan.

- Drinking lots of water and/or diet drinks to create a feeling of fullness.

- Threatening to be, or actually being, sick after a meal.

- Hiding food in clothes.

- Hiding food in the bedroom.

- Storing food in cheeks and then leaving the table to spit it out.

- Blowing nose at the meal table and spitting food into the tissue.

The bottom line is that anorexics will do anything to minimise their daily calorie intake. A young boy afflicted by anorexia might appear to be consuming 3,000 calories a day when in fact he is only consuming 1,000. The anorexia is constantly telling him not to eat. He will have no problem lying to you about what he has eaten or adopting some of the strategies mentioned above. If you believe your son is eating 3,000 calories a day, yet he is still losing weight, it is likely that he is either vomiting or he is just creating an illusion of eating a healthy diet.

You cannot make your son eat, but as a carer and provider of his daily needs you can adopt some strategies that will encourage him to eat sensibly and discourage him from the rituals and habits mentioned above:

- Try to have meals as a family so that eating becomes a social situation rather than just about food. Of course this is not always possible in today's hectic family lives, but even if families just eat together at the weekends this is preferable than not at all. Try to avoid situations where your anorexic son is able to eat alone.

- Try to make meals a fun time in which members of the family recount stories from their day, talk about the latest film, soap, football match or anything else that is light-hearted and not about food. We also found that playing a game of cards after a meal was a good way of keeping Joe at the table long enough for his meal to settle. Ensure that the rest of the family understand why they shouldn't talk about food at the table and that it is especially important that they don't comment on how much your son has eaten or not eaten. For example, a well-meaning granny can cause a huge amount of upset by commenting on how well or badly your son has done at a meal.

- Avoid confrontation at mealtimes. If you notice that your son is pushing food off his plate, spitting it into tissues or any of the other habits mentioned above, it is best to wait until after the meal. Later, perhaps at bedtime, you can let him know that you have seen what he is doing. Explain (again and again if necessary) why you want him to eat and gain weight. Be very loving and supportive. Tell him that you understand how difficult it is for him to eat a proper meal. Give him lots of praise for the progress he has made so far, but gently let him know that he can do better. It is unlikely that he will be able to give up his rituals straight away, but with lots of support he may gradually be able to let them go one at a time.

- Don't let your anorexic son prepare meals for himself or for the rest of the family. He is likely to overfeed everyone else and underfeed himself. Explain to him that once he has reached a reasonable weight he will be able to take more responsibility for his food intake. If you are preparing his food and he is eating it in front of you then you will have a much clearer idea of how much is actually being consumed.

- If your son gets into the habit of saying he is going to be sick because you have made him eat too much you might consider giving him a bowl at the table. It is unlikely that he will want to use it in front of everyone else. Many anorexics will threaten to be sick, but will never carry out that threat.

- When your son is at school it is impossible for you to see what he is eating. Depending on his age and/or social circle it might be appropriate to ask the teaching staff or one of his friends to keep an eye on his eating habits at school. You might also consider asking the school to provide special meals. For example, some anorexics are happy to eat a jacket potato and beans, but will not eat a roast lunch. In addition if he is on a re-feeding programme he will need to be served up larger portions. In some cases it is useful to tell your son this is happening, in others it might put him off eating at school altogether. We discussed with Joe various options including having special meals, sitting in a separate room with a couple of friends and taking a packed lunch to school. In the end he decided he would rather come home for lunch as he felt this was the most discreet option. Despite the fact that he was already very ill, he couldn't face his peers seeing him have special treatment at lunchtime.

There is a huge element of trial and error when it comes to eating with your anorexic son. What works for one family may not work for another. The most important thing is to try and make your son feel relaxed about mealtimes, avoid confrontation, and give him as much support and encouragement as you can. Don't be disheartened when there are setbacks, take a deep breath and carry on.

Exercise

Joe was a very sporty and active boy before he developed anorexia. At the beginning he felt that if he ate a little less and did a little more exercise he would become an even better sportsman. However, after a few weeks he became obsessive about exercising more and more. He insisted on going to every after school activity which involved exercise. He was particularly keen on swimming club and athletics club because he could work really hard in them. Initially, his swimming and athletics coaches were both very pleased with the results he was achieving. However, within a few weeks they both became concerned about his rapid weight loss and his obsessive determination to do better and better. A month later Joe had become so weak he couldn't carry on with these clubs, but he soon replaced his sporting activity at school with repetitive exercise at home. On a typical day he would do:

- 100 sit-ups or more after every meal and extra in the evening

- 50 press-ups or more after every meal and extra in the evening

- 20 pull-ups or more every time he went up or down the stairs

- 20 pull-ups or more every time he walked down the hallway

- several hard work-outs on the exercise bike

- constant tensing of his stomach muscles as well as flexing his arm and leg muscles

- constant tapping of his feet if he wasn't actually exercising – he couldn't bear to be still for a minute.

These are the exercises we were aware of. It is likely he was doing other exercises in his bedroom. Anorexics have been known to set their alarm clocks for the middle of the night so that they can do more secret exercise whilst everyone else is asleep.

Stopping your son exercising is at least as difficult as trying to encourage him to eat. Normal sporty active boys will exercise a lot more than their non-sporty counterparts. It is almost impossible to know where to draw the line. In addition if your son has got to the stage where he is obsessively exercising at every opportunity, then it is unlikely that he will be able to stop without some outside professional help. The more you try to dissuade him from exercising the more likely he is to exercise in secret.

Excessive compulsive exercising can be very dangerous for anyone, but more so for a growing boy. Exercise puts strain on a heart already weakened by starvation; muscles become severely wasted and can no longer support the joints, which can become badly damaged.

It is important to try to dissuade your son from obsessive repetitive exercising. You might consider trying some of the following strategies:

- Explain that the normal recommendation for children and adults is that they should exercise for about 20 minutes three times a week. Of course athletes do a lot more than this, but they are supervised by qualified coaches and have qualified physiotherapists available to deal with any injuries.

- Watch your son carefully. He may tell you he has stopped exercising and instead be exercising in the bathroom, at night or anywhere else that you cannot see.

- Tell your son that if he continues to do so much exercise then he needs to see a doctor to assess his physical condition. This in itself might be a good deterrent.

- If this doesn't achieve the desired effect, then carry through the threat to go to the doctor. The doctor might be able to persuade him to reduce his exercising regime or he might feel it is appropriate to refer your son onto a specialist. At the very least he should check his weight and physical observations such as pulse and heart rate.

If your son has lost weight and continues to exercise obsessively, it is important to seek professional medical help before he does himself too much long-term physical damage.

Rituals

Joe developed many rituals, as he became more and more ill. It was as if he was frightened that if he didn't carry out his daily rituals something terrible would happen. These are some of the rituals he developed:

- counting on his fingers throughout the day
- touching walls and surfaces as he walked around the house
- chewing his knuckles until they bled
- touching and/or walking around dustbins in the town and park
- picking up other people's litter, however disgusting it might be
- obsessive hand washing throughout the day
- strict routine of personal hygiene every evening at the same time
- keeping his bedroom spotless
- reading his children's bible out loud
- tracing the lines in his bible with his finger
- stepping over the room divides and cracks in the pavement
- shuffling up and down stairs one step at a time
- constant eye tic
- dragging one foot as he walked
- writing in a very flowery and elaborate manner.

When I asked him why he did these things he simply replied that it made him feel better. I wondered whether I should try and discourage Joe from doing them but concluded that they weren't doing Joe or anyone else any harm. I hoped that once he had regained weight he would lose the compulsion to do them and for the most part this happened very quickly. Six months after his discharge from the residential unit he was still touching surfaces, but all the other rituals had gone. I discussed this with Joe's psychiatrist who agreed it wasn't doing any harm. He advised me to keep an eye out for any other obsessive traits developing, but they never did. Soon after, Joe stopped touching surfaces of his own accord.

In most cases the development of ritualistic behaviour is directly related to weight loss and ongoing starvation. Whilst it might be distressing to watch it is often harmless. If any aspect of your son's behaviour is harmful in any way or upsetting for other family members then of course it should be discouraged. It might be useful to set boundaries for acceptable behaviour. For example, if your son is spending so much time in the bathroom in the morning that everyone else is late for school or work, then this behaviour is unacceptable. Rather than having a huge fight every day it is easier to give your son guidance as to what is acceptable. A gentle approach is likely to deliver the best outcome:

> 'I understand why you feel you need to spend more time in the bathroom at the moment, but other people need to use it as well. You can use the bathroom any time up until 7 am, but then it must be available for the rest of the family. I love you very much, but it is not acceptable that you are making everyone else late in the morning because you want to spend so long in the shower.'

Weight

By definition anorexics are obsessed with their weight. Many will weigh themselves several times a day. Because everyone weighs a little more later in the day (500 g to 1 kg) anorexics often become depressed as the number on the scale increases. This can then be a huge deterrent to them eating later on in the day.

Weight is just as much of an obsession in the recovery phase. Your son might have agreed to embark on a re-feeding plan to gain weight, but will still be absolutely terrified of actually gaining weight. You might have agreed that he should be weighed once a week to monitor his progress. Many will try to boost their weight artificially for the once weekly weighing to try and fool you that they are putting on weight. Many will also argue that after appearing to have gained a very small amount of weight they are now much fatter than all their friends are.

Some common weighing tricks include:

- hiding heavy objects in pockets
- wearing heavy shoes and/or clothes
- drinking litres of water pre-weighing.

The last trick is very common and can also be very dangerous. It can quickly upset the delicate balance of salts in the body leading to dizziness and fainting, and excessive drinking can cause the brain to swell.

As a carer of an anorexic boy it is extremely important to have a clear idea of how his weight is changing, both up and down. If you are weighing him at home try to adopt a consistent approach:

- Aim to weigh him once a week.

- Weigh him at the same time of day, as we all get a little heavier as the day progresses.

- Always weigh him in the same place. Scales can show quite a different weight on different floor surfaces or if the floor is uneven.

- Weigh him in his underwear or a swimsuit to ensure he is not adding heavy objects.

- Observe him carefully to ensure he is not water drinking to boost his weight. However this is the hardest trick to monitor and the only way to really check if he is water drinking is to carry out random spot checks at least once a week.

- Some anorexics find it extremely distressing to see their weight rising and so in some cases it is appropriate to weigh them blind. You can do this by getting them to stand backwards on the scales.

- Some families find it easier if the anorexic child is weighed outside the home, such as at the health centre or at school. If this is the case then make sure the same basic rules for weighing are applied. Whilst many school nurses and practice nurses are well aware of anorexic tricks, many are not.

Clothes

The fashion today is for children to wear big baggy clothes. This suits anorexics perfectly. They can hide their hated bodies under layers and layers of baggy clothes. This also serves the purpose of helping to keep them warm. Because they wear such baggy clothes it is often impossible to visually judge how much weight they have lost.

It is clear that anorexics hide their bodies beneath their clothes. Many parents of severely anorexic children have been fooled by this tactic and the child's anorexia has been allowed to develop unchallenged. Remember, the earlier the illness is diagnosed, the recovery is likely to be easier and more successful. Don't fall into the clothes trap yourselves.

Whilst many teenagers hide their developing bodies from the rest of the family, it is important for carers of an anorexic boy to try and see for themselves how emaciated he has become. An easy way to do this is to take the family swimming. If this option is refused and your son will simply not undress in front of you, even to be weighed, then you may have to revert to the visit to the doctor as described in the section on exercise above.

Moods, tantrums and irrational behaviour

Whilst it is emotionally draining watching your son starve himself and physically decline before your eyes, it is the psychological changes that can be the most difficult to deal with. All families quarrel, we all lose our temper at times, but an anorexic child can blow up into a frightening rage at the slightest incident. Anorexic tantrums and rages can be totally unpredictable. Often families with an anorexic in their midst end up tiptoeing around the house, trying to avoid upsetting the anorexic child and triggering yet another torrent of verbal abuse and upset.

In the same way that an anorexic boy might threaten to throw up if you make him eat too much, he is likely to make other even more alarming threats if you make him do something else he doesn't feel like doing. It might be a fairly major issue that you have raised which he finds frightening such as:

- I think you should stop doing sport and exercise until you start eating more.

- I am going to take you to see the doctor about your illness.

- We need to consider sending you to an in-patient unit for treatment.

On the other hand it might be a simple daily task you have asked him to do such as:

- I want you to tidy your bedroom.

- You need to do your homework.

- Can you help me clear the table?

In response to your latest request he might fly into a rage and tell you:

- You are ruining my life.

- You don't understand.

- You are not listening to me.

- You don't care about me.

- You don't love me.

Common threats include:

- I'm going to run away.

- I'm going to cut, burn or self-harm in some way.

- I'm going to kill myself.

These threats are frightening and if you believe that he has any intention of carrying them out it is important to see your doctor and get an emergency referral to a child psychiatrist. Some anorexics have such low self-esteem and feel so out of control that they do revert to self-harm and even suicide. Fortunately the numbers who actually attempt suicide are very low. Self-harm is more common and you should be on the look out for the appearance of unexplained cuts, burns and bruises. Children who do self-harm often say it helps relieve the stress they are feeling.

In many cases the anorexic child has no intention of carrying out these threats. Joe threatened to kill himself by jumping out of his bedroom window at his in-patient unit on several occasions when I refused to discharge him. Having read about typical behaviour of patients recently admitted to such units I knew that such threats were fairly common. Of course I was extremely worried that he might carry out his threats but at the time he was under very close observation by the staff and he wasn't allowed up to his bedroom on his own. He was extremely upset about being admitted to the unit, he was scared that the staff would make him fat and so was driven to saying anything in his desperate attempt to persuade me to take him home.

In his starvation induced irrational state of mind, your anorexic son might also do things that affect the rest of the family and are totally unacceptable. Very often he is simply seeking yet more attention. For example:

- He might take an older sibling's clothes, DVDs, CDs and so on, without asking and with no intention of giving them back.

- He might break a younger sibling's toys, especially if they are annoying him.

- He might break other household items just to get attention.

- He might lash out at other members of the family, either physically or verbally.

All of these actions are likely to cause upset and are not acceptable.

It is important to recognise that your son is ill and it is the anorexia, which is leading him to behave in this unpredictable and irrational way. However, it is also important to try and set him boundaries of behaviour that he can understand. He needs firm guidance and someone to try and take control. We eventually realised that tiptoeing around and trying to ignore Joe's behaviour was like giving in to the anorexia and letting it take control of the whole family. A gentle but firm approach was the best way of coping with his behaviour:

- Arguing back and shouting simply adds fuel to the fire.

- Keep reminding yourself to stay calm.

- Remember that some things aren't worth arguing about, it might be best to walk away if he isn't upsetting the rest of the family by his behaviour.

If his behaviour is affecting the rest of the family try approaches such as:

- I love you very much and I know it is the anorexia making you do this but it is not acceptable to the rest of the family when you do this and I want you to try really hard not to do it again.

- How would you feel if your brother or sister did this to your things? In future if you are feeling upset about something I would like you to come to me and talk about it.

Sometimes these approaches will have the desired effect. Other times they might not, but it is important not to give up. Take a deep breath and carry on trying to give your son as much support and guidance as possible. He needs your help to try to take control of the anorexia.

It is very stressful trying to keep some sense of normality in your household when you have an anorexic child within your midst. The anorexia is very powerful and will use every opportunity to take control of the whole family. Try to remember that whilst you cannot control what the anorexia is doing to your son, you can control how it affects you and the rest of the family. In addition with lots of love and support you can help your son start to take control back from his anorexia.

6. Effects on the family

Anorexia is a very manipulative illness, and families that try to ignore its existence can soon find that the anorexia is controlling the lives of all the individuals within the family. By working together, a family unit can be very successful in taking control of the anorexia and helping the sufferer overcome his difficulties with eating. I mention later on that family therapy often forms a key part of a successful treatment programme.

The main carer is very often the mother, but could be the father, an older sibling or another close relative. For the purposes of this section I have assumed it is the mother. It is likely that the main carer will have been proactive in finding out more about eating disorders, and whilst this has inevitably created a feeling of panic, she is more able to understand the feelings her son might be having. This may not be the case for other members of the family.

Because all families are different I cannot cover every possible effect that anorexia is likely to have on every different family situation. However, there are some common situations that are worth considering. They illustrate the sort of issues families may face when one member becomes anorexic.

My spouse/partner doesn't understand

This seems to be a very common comment by the main carer of an anorexic child. Consider the situation where the husband comes home from a busy day at work. He walks in to find his wife and son having yet another debate about food. His wife is very distressed, but is trying to calmly explain to her son why he needs to eat. His son is still refusing to eat. The husband thinks this behaviour is ridiculous and shouts at his son, telling him he must sit down and eat his dinner. His son flies into a violent rage, accusing both parents of all sorts of terrible things and then walks out of the room, slamming the door behind him. The wife bursts into tears and tells the husband he shouldn't shout at their son because it will only make things worse. The husband says he can't understand why his son is being so ridiculous about food and it is about time someone made him eat. Everyone ends up being very upset and cross with each other. The son has managed to avoid yet another meal.

There are several reasons why this sort of scene has been experienced by many families faced with an anorexic child:

- Men and women react to things in different ways and express their feelings in different ways. This can lead to conflict in many areas of family life.

- The husband knows nothing about eating disorders, he thinks his son is being a difficult teenager, he thinks his wife is being too weak and can't understand why she doesn't just take control and make him eat.

- The wife is exhausted. She feels she is fighting a losing battle both with her son's anorexia and her husband's attitude to it. She feels she is totally alone.

- The fact that the parents are disagreeing in front of their son gives him the opportunity to play one off against the other. This is a great way to fuel his anorexia further. His anorexia is taking control of the family, rather than the family taking control of the anorexia.

What can you do to avoid this sort of situation occurring?

- **Education**. It is very difficult when only one of the carers understands the illness that the son is suffering from. If both carers (and indeed any other adults living within the family group) learn everything they can about anorexia then it makes it much easier to share the burden and tackle the problem together.

- **Communication**. This is essential if both carers are going to work together to help their son overcome his illness. They must agree on the approach to be taken and both communicate the same message to their son. An anorexic needs structure and if his carers disagree in front of him on the right approach to be taken, he will feel confused and lost. Anorexia will then take control of the situation. Sometimes it helps if you can put aside a set time each week when you and your partner can sit down and discuss how things are progressing. It might be appropriate to include your son and/or other members of the family, but this depends entirely on the individual circumstance.

- **Avoid conflict and rows**. It is unbelievably stressful living with an anorexic child. Sometimes you cannot help shouting either at your spouse or your anorexic child. However, this almost never has a positive outcome. It is important for both carers to try to be calm with each other and with the anorexic child. He needs firm guidance from both carers given in a calm and logical manner.

My other child has become very withdrawn

This is a natural response to a sibling's anorexia and my younger son did exactly this. Siblings will probably notice at an early stage that their brother is not his usual self. They will probably have picked up that their mother is anxious and their father is cross. They may also feel that the anorexic son is getting more than his fair share of his parents' attention at the moment. Withdrawing to the bedroom is the easiest option in such a situation.

As with the first scenario, education and communication can help enormously. Obviously it depends on the age of the siblings as to how much you tell them about the illness and its effect on their brother. What is important is to make sure they feel involved and don't feel they are being pushed aside by their brother's illness. Children who feel they are not getting enough attention from their parents may start to have problems at school. They may not be able to concentrate and so their grades might start to suffer. They might start to misbehave either at home or at school in order to get more attention. They might start to comfort eat, or they might copy their brother's behaviour and cut down on food themselves.

It is well worth trying to spend some special time with your other children on their own, maybe a trip to the cinema or a shopping trip and a meal. You might like to ask them how they are feeling or explain your concerns about your son and see how they respond. It is important for the siblings to feel secure within the family. If you make them feel included and explain what is happening they will be more relaxed. They may even have some useful insights as to what is going on in your anorexic son's mind at the moment.

If you feel your other children's schoolwork is being affected it is important to let an appropriate person at the school know why. The last thing you want is your other children becoming miserable because their teachers are putting pressure on them.

My eldest son/daughter wants to leave home

If you have older teenage children they may resent the extra attention that your anorexic son is getting so much that they threaten to leave home. It might be the natural time for them to go anyway or you might feel it is totally inappropriate. Once again education and communication are crucial. You may well find that the elder sibling actually decides to stay at home to give moral support to the rest of the family. In other cases they may decide to go anyway, but at least if they understand your son's illness they are less likely to feel that they have been driven out of their home by it.

My anorexic son is trying to make the rest of the family fat

This can happen for two reasons:

1. It is very common for an anorexic to try to persuade everyone around him to eat more food. It makes him feel even more proud of his ability

to restrict his own food intake. My son used to be forever offering his younger brother biscuits and Mars bars. Other anorexics have been known to make elaborate meals, give everyone enormous helpings, but only have a tiny portion themselves.

2. If your son is on a re-feeding diet, by definition he will have to eat more than everyone else in the family to gain weight. If he can persuade everyone else to eat more he will feel less guilty about finishing his own meal.

This is unacceptable behaviour and the carers must try to put a stop to it as soon as possible. Both the anorexic child and his siblings need to be given clear guidance on what is acceptable when it comes to food. The easiest way to stop this sort of behaviour is to restrict your son's access to the kitchen while he is ill. If the carers take control of dishing up meals and handing out snacks to the other siblings then this situation should be easily avoided. However, once your son is well on the way to recovery it will be appropriate to let him start to take some responsibility for his own food intake and to let him have access to the kitchen.

My other relatives are interfering

For some families the extended family can be a godsend. Helpful relatives will step in from time to time to give the carers and other siblings a break. The anorexic child might find it easier to express his feelings to a favourite uncle or granny and that could be key to helping him over his illness.

Unfortunately, for many families the extended family insists on interfering and making unhelpful comments such as:

- He's always been a difficult child.

- Mental illness runs in the family.

- Once an anorexic always an anorexic.

- You shouldn't have sent him to that childminder/ boarding school and so on.

- You gave him too much freedom.

- You didn't give him enough freedom.

It is stressful enough looking after an anorexic child and the rest of your family without having this sort of external pressure. It is important to decide at an early stage who you want to be involved and who you don't. Encourage your helpful relatives to learn as much as they can about the illness and they may then be in a position to be extremely helpful. Try to discourage those who are prone to making negative comments from getting involved. You might have to be incredibly thick skinned and/or blunt, but you don't need extra pressure from interfering relatives.

There is no doubt that anorexia affects the whole family. Some members may be affected more than others. Some might not be affected at all. What is important is that the whole family works together to try and help the sufferer pull through. Some families might find it easy to sit down and talk about their problems and/or issues and come up with a plan of action to resolve them. Most families don't find this easy. Family therapy is a very useful way of bringing a family together for a set time on a regular basis. Family therapists are trained to help the family identify issues and to set about resolving them. It is not easy to accept that your family might benefit from family therapy, but for many families it has been an invaluable tool in helping one of their family members get over anorexia. This topic is dealt with in more detail in Chapter 9.

7.   Self-help

In the preceding chapters I have described living with an anorexic boy and the effects on the family, and offered some practical tips that you might try when dealing with all the stresses and strains that anorexia has brought into your home. You and your family are probably feeling exhausted and isolated by your son's illness. However much your wider family and friends want to help, they cannot really understand what you as a family are going through if they have no direct experience of anorexia itself. Undoubtedly some of you will have been subjected to well-meaning comments such as:

- I'm sure it's a passing phase.

- He's always been a bit fussy about food hasn't he?

- He's just having typical teenage tantrums.

- Lots of boys go through skinny phases.

These comments might be well-meaning but they can be very upsetting when you know deep down that there is something much more serious wrong with your son. It is at this stage that you might consider seeking outside help from people who have a great deal of experience with eating disorders. Help can come from many sources, but basically comes under two headings:

1. Self-help.

2. Help from the medical profession.

In this chapter, I describe the self-help options. In Chapters 8 and 9, I describe what the medical profession has to offer.

The Eating Disorder Association (EDA) is the leading charity in the UK offering information, help and support to anyone affected by eating disorders. The EDA offers a range of services, which include:

- telephone helplines

- UK wide network of self-help and support groups, postal, email and telephone contacts

- membership which includes a regular newsletter

- a comprehensive range of information, including leaflets for young people

- lists of specialist treatment centres available around the country
- an annual conference for members to get together and learn about the latest developments.

The EDA website (www.edauk.com) contains details of all these services as well as providing a very useful recommended reading list.

The EDA can offer a great deal of support to both the sufferers and carers affected by an eating disorder. Simply by calling the telephone helpline you are making the first step towards self-help. The person at the other end of the line understands what you are going through and can offer a sympathetic ear and many good words of advice. Suddenly you realise that you are not alone!

Self-help can also include joining a support group or communicating with others who have experienced eating disorders by post or email.

At an EDA annual conference in 2001 the benefits of self-help were summarised and included:

- reduction in isolation – a feeling of not being alone
- opportunities for sharing experiences and coping skills
- mutual support – the opportunity for talking to people who have 'been there'
- swapping and learning new, practical ways of dealing with problems
- better understanding of own health concern/social issues
- feeling empowered to take positive steps towards a better health/ social situation
- taking an active role in own health/well-being
- a feeling of being more in control
- increased self-esteem
- increased self-confidence
- alleviation of stress
- reduction in fear and anxiety
- the provision of relevant information and literature
- gaining inspiration and support from others' experience
- alleviation of stress
- an opportunity to give as well as receive help

- increase in social opportunities/social circle
- development of new skills.

These are all fairly compelling reasons why it is well worth contacting a self-help organisation such as the EDA.

As I have already mentioned the EDA offers help and support for both sufferers and carers. It is worth mentioning exactly what they can offer your son as a young sufferer, as well as what they can offer you as a carer.

The youth section of the EDA

The EDA youth team aims to offer help, advice and support to young people who are 18 years of age and under. If you can persuade your son to make contact with the team this could be a first important step towards recovery. The EDA has produced a booklet entitled: *Information About Eating Disorders, A Guide For Young People.*

It is a very welcoming introduction to the youth section of the EDA and what it has to offer. It explains what eating disorders are and how to get help. It also gives information on a young person's entitlement to confidentiality. Importantly it contains several pictures of young boys acknowledging that boys get eating disorders too!

It also provides details of how to contact the EDA youthline and email service, which is called 'talkback'. The EDA also has a message board where you can just read what others have said or participate by sending your own message. The EDA youthline telephone number is 0845 634 7650 and you can contact talkback on talkback@edauk.com.

Of course there are other organisations that offer help for young people and your son might find it helpful to contact such organisations as ChildLine or YoungMinds either by phone or on their websites.

ChildLine is a free 24-hour helpline for children and young people in the UK. Children and young people can call the helpline on 0800 1111 about any problem, at any time – day or night, or look on the website at www.childline.org.uk

YoungMinds is a national charity committed to improving the mental health of all children and young people. YoungMinds produces leaflets and booklets to help young people, parents and professionals to understand when a young person feels troubled and where to find help. YoungMinds have recently published a booklet entitled *Worried About Eating Disorders?* aimed at 11 to 16 year olds. Their website can be found at www.youngminds.org.

uk. The YoungMinds Parents' Information Service (0800 018 2138) provides information and advice for anyone with concerns about the mental health of a child or young person.

Unfortunately joining a self-help group may not be an option for your son if he is under 18 years of age, although some groups will allow 16 and 17 year olds to attend if accompanied by an adult. This could be an older sibling or friend. It doesn't have to be the parent or carer.

Help if your son is an athlete

In recent years there has been a growing recognition that young athletes can be susceptible to developing eating disorders. Certainly Joe felt that if he restricted his diet he would become an even better athlete.

Runner's World 'Buddy Scheme' is a self-help support network, which can put you in contact with sports psychologists and sports dieticians. You can contact them at 7-10 Chandos Street, London W1M OAD.

The EDA, in conjunction with the Runner's World Buddy Scheme, has put together a series of leaflets on eating disorders in athletes, which are available from the EDA. There are three leaflets in the series aimed at:

1. Athletes.

2. Coaches.

3. Friends and Family.

Self-help for carers

The EDA and other self-help organisation also offer a wide range of services for carers of young people with eating disorders. I include more on this in Chapter 11, Caring for the carer.

There are other self-help organisations that you might like to contact, such as Anorexia and Bulimia Care (ABC). It is a Christian organisation run by Christians for sufferers, their families and for carers in the UK. You can visit the Anorexia and Bulimia Care website at www.anorexiabulimiacare.co.uk

The key message of this chapter is that **you are not alone**. There is plenty of support out there and it is well worth making the effort to make contact with other people who have been through similar experiences. Self-help might sound daunting at first but the benefits are enormous. There is already a well-established self-help network in the UK and it is growing all the time.

8.   Treatment options

The UK Government confirmed its commitment to providing better treatment services for eating disorder sufferers when it commissioned the National Institute for Clinical Excellence (NICE) to produce guidelines for the treatment of eating disorders, based on the best available researched evidence and expert opinion. The guideline was published in January 2004 and has set the standard for NHS treatment. Whilst there are still huge variations in the availability of specialist treatment in different areas around the country, this was a major step forward in establishing acceptable treatment regimes for eating disorder sufferers. I refer to the guideline throughout this chapter.

There is a wide range of treatment options. While many young people with anorexia respond well to out-patient care, in-patient care is necessary when an eating disorder has led to physical problems that may be life-threatening, or when an eating disorder has reached a level where psychological or behavioural problems are severe. Many of the effects of anorexia are physical, but many are psychological. Treatment of anorexia must address both issues, and most treatment regimens include a combination of re-feeding to regain a normal body weight and a range of therapies to address the underlying issues. I have outlined some of the treatment options later on, but first it is worth pointing out two of the findings from the Eating Disorder Association (EDA) review of the provision of healthcare services for men with eating disorders which was published in 2000:

1. Men find it hard to acknowledge they have an eating disorder and then to seek help.

2. It is clear that the general lack of recognition of eating disorders in men makes it more difficult for them to access specialist eating disorder services. Their problems are less likely to be recognised and diagnosed by professionals including GP's and psychiatrists and therefore their illness may be well established before treatment is offered.

These findings certainly coincide with our experience. Not only did Joe find it difficult to acknowledge that he had an eating disorder, we also felt it was unlikely because, 'boys don't get anorexia do they?' In addition our GP, our friends and the teachers at school found it difficult to believe that this 12-year-old boy could have an eating disorder. Only when Joe was very ill did we finally all agree that he had anorexia.

An important message to parents or carers of a boy who looks as if he may have an eating disorder is: **don't wait for too long before seeking specialist help.**

As I have already explained in Chapter 1, growing boys who restrict their diet can do themselves a great deal of long-term damage. Early treatment is likely to have the best outcome in the shortest time, but even then full recovery is likely to take at least a year. Patients with established eating disorders may well take at least five years to recover. By the time you as a parent/carer starts to worry that your son has an eating disorder, his condition is likely to have already started to become established. Weight is one of the key indicators. A teenage boy who doesn't gain any weight over a three-month period may well be restricting his diet and alarm bells should start ringing. A teenage boy who is actually losing weight should see a GP as a matter of urgency. In any event, if you have been unsuccessful in trying to persuade your son to eat a sensible diet and he continues to restrict his food intake it is vital to seek professional specialist help. Joe managed to lose 25% of his body weight in just four months. In the end he nearly suffered a heart attack and his pulse and blood pressure had dropped to dangerously low levels.

Whether you choose to use the NHS or go privately, your first port of call is your GP. However, be warned that many GP's have little or no experience about eating disorders. The UK Government's NICE guideline says that, 'People with eating disorders seeking help should be assessed and receive treatment at the earliest opportunity.' However, hardly a week goes by without the Eating Disorder Association (EDA) hearing from a family whose story includes the fact that their GP either didn't pick up on the problem or didn't act quickly enough.

To maximise the likelihood of an early diagnosis being made, you need to go armed with enough facts about the deterioration in your son's health that your GP will sit up and take notice. There are three key things your GP is likely be interested in and which will help him to recognise that your son might be suffering from anorexia:

1. How much weight has your son lost and over what time period?

2. How has his behaviour changed and has he developed any rituals or unusual habits?

3. What have you tried at home to reverse the weight loss and why do you think this has not succeeded?

It is very likely that your son will deny he has a problem with eating. He may claim that all the boys in his class are equally skinny, and if the doctor suggests to him that he should try to eat a bit more 'if only to keep his mum happy', he is likely to promise the doctor that he will do that. If your son's physical observations, such as pulse and blood pressure, are within the normal range it is very likely that the doctor will send you home to give your son a chance to fulfil his promise of eating more. Don't be disheartened. Give your son a chance to prove he can change his eating pattern. If he doesn't, then go back to your GP a week later. If necessary keep going back once a week, either until your son has improved his eating habits or until your GP takes notice. If your son has anorexia he will very quickly lose more weight, which should help your GP to be more sympathetic. My doctor suggested that I was a fussy mum when I first approached him with concerns about Joe, but later on, when he could see that Joe's health was deteriorating, he was invaluable in referring us on to the specialists qualified to treat patients with eating difficulties.

A GP with knowledge of eating disorders, or who has healthcare professionals with these skills within the practice, might suggest an initial plan of action that involves caring for your son at home with the help of this professional expertise. This could include a dietician or nurse therapist providing basic nutritional and health education, perhaps with referral to a local eating disorder self-help group. It is very often the case that a teenager, who refuses to listen to his parents, will listen very carefully to a warning from a GP or nurse over the dangers of severely restricting food intake over a period of time.

Unfortunately, in the UK not many GP's have sufficient knowledge of eating disorders or are in practices that are lucky enough to employ eating disorder specialists. In most cases the GP will refer your son on to a paediatrician and/ or child psychiatrist for further assessment.

Involvement of parents/carers in the treatment of young people

Before describing the specialist treatment options it is worth considering the issue of how involved parents/carers should be in the treatment of young people with eating disorders. All too often parents are actually excluded, or feel that they are being unnecessarily excluded, from their child's treatment regime and the EDA help-line receives many calls from frustrated parents on this subject.

Different therapy teams have different views on how involved parents should be. In particular, therapy teams who are not used to dealing with young people with eating disorders may not appreciate how important it is for the family to be involved in the treatment and recovery process. Some therapy teams hide behind the issue of confidentiality and seek to exclude the parents in order to protect their patient's confidentiality. The NICE guideline supports involving families and carers, but it does point out that every individual has rights of confidentiality. Young people with eating disorders might be having difficulties in their family life and in some cases there may have been familial abuse, which has contributed to the eating disorder. A young person has to trust his therapy team not to go running back to his parents with every comment that he makes. The therapy process that an eating disorder patient goes through can be very painful and very private to the individual and there is no reason why his parents should be privy to every detail. The NICE guideline states that confidentiality should only be broken if the patient or others are deemed to be at significant risk and where informing the parent is likely to reduce that risk. However, whilst confidentiality is clearly an important issue, it should not be used as a reason to exclude parents altogether.

The NICE guideline considers this a very important issue and states that the families of young people being treated for an eating disorder should be involved in their treatment and care. This is not because they are part of the problem, but because they are vital to the solution and can play a vital role in helping and supporting the young person on the long road to recovery.

The NICE guideline suggests that parents who are feeling left out, or are unsure what their role should be in the treatment process, should consider asking the patient's therapy team the following questions:

- What role can we have in helping the person with the eating disorder with their problem?

- Can you please let us know how the treatment of the person with the eating disorder is progressing?

- Can you advise us on the kind of support that you think we might benefit from as a family?

The NICE guideline goes on to say that parents/carers should be given enough information to help them provide care effectively. Respecting the patient's confidentiality should not be accepted as an excuse for excluding the parents or carers from being involved in the treatment process.

When our son was first admitted to an in-patient unit we felt excluded and were frustrated at the lack of communication. We felt that the more we asked questions, the more was being kept from us. In actual fact Joe's therapy team had very little to report in the first month. Joe was too ill to start therapy and he needed very close supervision from the nursing team to ensure his re-feeding programme didn't put too much pressure on his fragile body. Joe was angry and frustrated at the seemingly slow rate of progress and vented his anger at the family when we came to visit. This was all quite normal for a very sick anorexic child but we didn't know that. In time we got to know the therapy team and we started to understand that there is no magic cure for anorexia. The road to recovery is a long and slow one and everyone involved has to be extremely patient. Once we understood this it was much easier for us to have a useful dialogue with Joe's therapy team and we all worked together to ensure his recovery phase went as smoothly as possible.

What are the specialist treatment options?

Each case is different and there are many different treatment options. What is clear is that the earlier anorexia is recognised and treated, the quicker and less painful the route to recovery. Most patients may be successfully treated as out-patients, using some form of counselling approach and lots of family support. Depending on where you live and your son's physical and mental state your GP might refer your son to a:

- paediatrician
- child and adolescent psychiatric or mental health unit.

Paediatricians are medical doctors who specialise in diagnosing and treating illnesses in children and teenagers. The paediatrician will be able to give your son a thorough check-up and assess whether his eating disorder has caused, or is likely to cause, any medical problems. The paediatrician can also carry out a wide range of other tests to rule out any other illnesses. Once the paediatrician has diagnosed anorexia he is likely to refer your son to a child psychiatrist for further assessment. If your son is very ill he might recommend an emergency in-patient admission.

Child and adolescent psychiatric or mental health units specialise in dealing with psychological and behavioural problems in children and teenagers. You and/or your son might feel embarrassed about going to a psychiatric unit, but you should just try and view it as seeing another specialist doctor. If your son had a bad knee you would see a knee specialist. If he has psychological problems with eating then it is appropriate that he is seen by doctors, nurses and therapists trained in psychiatry and psychology. At this stage you and your son might meet with several different medical professionals and it can be very confusing. Each might have a different role to play in your son's assessment, treatment and recovery. In the course of your son's treatment you are likely to come across the following different types of professional:

- **Child psychiatrists**. These are medically qualified doctors who have specialised in the diagnosis and treatment of mental illness in children. A consultant psychiatrist is the senior member of the psychiatric team with overall responsibility for a patient's assessment and care.

- **Psychiatric nurses**. These are nurses who have specialist training in mental health. They work with hospital in-patients and with patients attending day centres and psychiatric units.

- **Community psychiatric or mental health nurses**. These are psychiatric nurses who work in the community rather than in hospitals. They may be attached to GP's surgeries, community mental health teams, mental health centres or psychiatric units. They may also visit your son at home. Their role includes offering emotional support and helping your son to explore ways of living with his issues around food. They can help with anxiety management techniques and can administer psychiatric drugs if appropriate.

- **Psychologists**. They have specialist postgraduate training but they are not medical doctors and do not prescribe drugs. They are highly trained to deal with human emotion and behaviour and can help with a variety of problems including eating difficulties, behavioural changes and depression. They will often suggest the therapy programme that they think will best suit your son's individual needs. This is likely to include individual therapy with the psychologist plus group therapy and a range of other therapies. The main types of therapy on offer are described in the next chapter.

- **Therapists**. They are trained to listen and will have a formal qualification in their chosen area. This might be psychotherapy, family therapy, cognitive behavioural therapy etc. The main aim of therapy is to give the patient time and space to explore important issues in their lives and to consider any changes which might be useful.

- **Dieticians/nutritionists**. They will offer your son (and you as carer) specific help with his diet. This may involve keeping a food diary or the dietician may provide you with specific diet sheets. It is important that you follow the dietician's advice carefully. The dietician will seek to re-educate your son about healthy eating and how much he needs to eat to achieve a reasonable weight. Some dieticians are more pro-active than others are, but if you do have access to a good dietician it is important to try and establish a good working relationship at an early stage. An experienced dietician can help your son overcome some of his problems with food and can help you construct a healthy diet for him that he will be willing to eat.

You can see from the above list that your son is likely to be seen by a range of professionals. A psychiatrist, nurse, therapist or clinical psychologist might undertake counselling and therapy. As long as the practitioner is adequately trained and experienced in dealing with eating disorders, it doesn't really matter what their title is.

Out-patient treatment might be undertaken at your local hospital, a Child and Adolescent Psychiatric Unit, your local health centre, a specialist day centre or at home. It depends on the location and availability of the doctors, nurses and therapists involved in your son's care. If his mood and weight start to lift, these are good signs that his treatment programme is working. If his weight continues to fall and/or his mood deteriorates then you should seek an urgent appointment with his consultant psychiatrist to consider altering his treatment programme. In any event you should have access to your son's professional team and there should be regular meetings scheduled to discuss progress. Don't be shy of asking questions or giving your opinions on how well or badly your son is doing. The medical team only sees your son during the day and for specific sessions. You are the only person who sees the whole picture and your input to his treatment programme is extremely important.

In-patient treatment is also available, both within hospitals and in independent specialist units. In-patient treatment is normally suitable for patients:

- who have suffered an extreme and life threatening level of weight loss

- where the condition has become deeply ingrained over a number of years and perhaps has a significant obsessional element

- where the patient is suffering from other disorders which may be life threatening such as suicidal tendencies and self-harm.

A main priority is re-feeding, with appropriate therapy following on when the patient is stronger. In-patient treatment is often a lengthy process lasting anywhere from 3 to 12 months.

If your son is admitted to an in-patient unit he will be treated by the same group of professionals as mentioned above. Progress might seem slow at first, but remember that your son has been admitted because he is very ill. Joe had to sit quietly for a month and even then he was only allowed a tiny amount of activity every day. He was very frustrated and angry, but if he had been more active he could have had a heart attack. In the second part of this book I describe in detail Joe's experience as an in-patient. Different treatment centres might adopt slightly different strategies but the overall aims are always the same:

- to achieve a reasonable weight for age and height

- to overcome the psychological issues with food and eating

- to resolve any other issues with anxiety and depression.

The advantages of your son being treated as an in-patient are that:

- his diet can be strictly controlled by the professional staff
- a wide range of therapies are available on a daily basis.

Many anorexics feel relieved when they are admitted to an in-patient unit. They no longer have to fight with their parents over every meal because an independent party has taken over. The anorexic voice doesn't seem so dominant in this situation. The medical staff at the unit have authority and it is rare for anorexics to refuse to eat. Many still have difficulty eating but they will at least sit at the table and try.

Whilst every in-patient unit is slightly different there are many things that are common including:

- **An expectation of weight gain**. Most units aim for a weight gain of between 0.5 to 1 kg per week. Your son's re-feeding programme is likely to include a build up phase in which he is given fairly small portions. This is to ensure that he doesn't adversely react to suddenly having much larger meals. His heart has been weakened by a long period of starvation and it is important to build up slowly. After several weeks it is likely that your son will be on a diet of over 3,000 calories per day. A dietician will work with the staff on duty to adjust his diet as necessary to ensure a reasonable and sustainable increase in weight.

- **Target weight**. At some stage your son will be given a target weight. Most units use boy's weight charts similar to the ones that are used to check the weight of a growing baby. These are often also referred to as centile charts. Joe's weight plummeted from being above the 50th centile to below the 9th centile in a few months. The target is likely to be set by the dietician involved in your son's care and it will take into account things such as how much he weighed before he was ill, how tall he is and his build. A small 12-year-old boy with a slight frame would be given a lower target weight than a tall 12-year-old boy with a large frame. Once your son has reached his target the unit will adjust his diet in order to stabilise his weight.

- **Predicted length of stay**. How long your son stays in the unit after this target has been reached depends on a wide range of factors including his mental state and how he has responded to therapy. Some units apply a formula to predict length of in-patient stay. For example, this might be one week per kg to be gained plus two weeks after that to stabilise weight. A boy who needs to gain 10 kg would have a predicted length of stay of 12 weeks. Of course if he didn't gain the weight or was still having difficulties with eating he would be expected to stay longer. Some units like to keep patients longer than others do, in the hope that a more lengthy stay will reduce the risk of relapse. At Joe's unit progress was monitored on a week by week basis and there was no specific prediction about length of stay. You should expect your son to stay at least three to four months. More complex cases might require much longer stays.

- **Availability of therapies**. To start with it is very likely that your son will be too weak and confused to be actively involved in therapies. However, as he gets stronger his medical team will put together a programme of therapies that they feel will suit your son. Joe didn't participate in therapy in any meaningful way for the first month of his admission. After that he participated in a wide range of therapies including one-to-one psychotherapy, group therapy, family therapy, cognitive behavioural therapy and art therapy.

- **A keyworker**. Most units will allocate one member of staff to be responsible for your son's day-to-day life on the unit. Very often this will be a psychologist who will be available as often as possible for your son to talk to. The keyworker should also be the parent/carer's main point of contact.

- **Regular updates on progress**. Most units will have a formal system for updating both the patient and their parents/carers on progress. At Joe's unit this was done on a weekly basis. Patients often get very anxious on update day and it is important to try to be reassuring even if your son has had a bad week. Each Wednesday Joe would be weighed and have a review discussion with his keyworker. Objectives would be set for the coming week. We were given feedback at our evening visit.

- **Professionals' meetings**. These are likely to happen at key stages in your son's treatment programme. All of the medical staff involved in your son's treatment will attend and it is common for one of your son's teachers and GP to be invited as well. These are stressful meetings both for the patient and the parent/carer. Key decisions will be made about ongoing therapy, permitted levels of activity, reintegration back into school, home visits, whether drugs might help the recovery process, timing of discharge etc. This is your main opportunity to really find out how well or badly the medical team think your son is doing.

- **Parents/carers' support group**. Most units will either run a parent/carers support group or be able to put you in contact with one. These are invaluable as they give you an opportunity to share your experiences with other families who have gone through, or are going through, similar situations. You can discuss the stresses and strains and the inevitable feelings of despair when trying to look after a sick child. You can also talk about coping strategies and share practical tips for dealing with what often seem to be impossible situations. Most importantly you can talk about recovery and hope for the future.

- **Schooling**. Most units will either have their own teaching staff or will send their patients to a day centre near by. Some work will be obtained from the patient's school and some general sessions will be organised. The idea is to keep patients ticking over. To start with they are unlikely to participate in lessons as they are too ill. When they do start to participate school hours are likely to be fairly short to ensure there is enough time for therapy sessions, basic medical checks to be carried out and other activities.

- **Activities for patients**. Most units will organise activities for patients. Day-to-day activities, which all patients can participate in, might include arts and crafts, singing and drama. Many units also offer more strenuous activities such as swimming, badminton, rounders and aerobics. Patients recently admitted are unlikely to be allowed to participate in such activities until they are much stronger although different units have different views on this. At the weekends and in the school holidays other activities such as trips to the cinema, a theme park, the ten-pin bowling alley or the seaside might also be on offer. At Joe's unit they took a cautious approach with regard to activities. Joe was not allowed to do any strenuous activity or to go on the outside trips until he had almost reached his target BMI. He found this extremely frustrating, but he had to learn to understand how sick he had made himself. Too much activity at an early stage could have triggered a heart attack. Most units will also exclude patients from activities if they are failing to gain weight or are thought to be exercising in secret.

- **Home visits**. Most units will discourage home visits for the first few weeks. It is important for the patient to settle in at the unit and get used to the strict regime. Once he is settled and complying with the unit's boundaries then home visits can be considered. Joe didn't come home at all in his first month at the unit. After that he only came home for a few hours at a time and he had to return to the unit for his meals. Gradually over the course of the second month he was allowed longer periods at home, introducing meals and finally staying overnight. Joe didn't come home for a whole weekend until he had nearly reached his target weight.

- **A word of warning**. It is very distressing for the whole family when one of its members goes into a residential unit for an unidentifiably long period of time. It takes time for everyone to adjust and the first few weeks are likely to be very difficult. It is not at all uncommon for a young person to become extremely distressed. Having happily gone along to the unit, he quickly finds out there are very strict rules and regulations. There is no choice about food and he has to sit with the other patients and eat everything that is given to him. Suddenly he realises he would prefer to be at home and he will try anything to achieve that objective. It is very common for new patients to ring home and make the following types of statement:

  - All the staff hate me and are really horrible.

  - I'm not like any of the other patients: you have sent me to the wrong place.

  - I promise I'll eat if you bring me home.

  - I'll commit suicide if you leave me here a minute longer.

  - If you love me you'll bring me home.

Being forewarned about this is being forearmed. Luckily we had read enough to know that such reactions were common. It didn't make the first few weeks any easier, but we were prepared for the emotional onslaught every time we visited or spoke to Joe on the phone. We could be strong and reassure Joe that we loved him very much and wanted him to get better. Staying at the unit was the best way of getting Joe back on the road to recovery.

In the UK there are both NHS specialist units and private clinics. Unfortunately there are many sufferers and not enough spaces to accommodate them all. If your son is very ill then your GP can apply for an emergency admission. This is what happened with Joe. In less urgent cases you might be able to get your son into a specialist unit on a daily basis. If you feel strongly that your son needs admission to a specialist unit don't give up. Keep taking him back to your GP, child psychologist or paediatrician and explain why you think he needs admission. Document any deterioration you have observed in his physical and/or mental state and make sure your son's medical team are well aware of these changes. If you still don't feel your son is being given the appropriate treatment, then it is worth seeking a second opinion even if this means changing to a new GP.

In-patient stays typically require a period of out-patient follow-up and aftercare to address the underlying issues in the individual's eating disorder, and to maximise the chances of avoiding a relapse. When Joe was discharged from his in-patient unit, he was transferred to the care of our local child and adolescent mental health unit. For the next six months Joe attended regular cognitive behavioural sessions at this unit, we all attended family therapy and Joe was seen by his consultant child psychiatrist every month or so. During that time Joe became much more relaxed about food, his weight rose steadily in accordance with his age and height, and his mood was good. Six months after leaving the in-patient unit, Joe was discharged from the care of the local child and adolescent mental health unit.

9. Therapy, therapy, therapy

Many people have never taken part in any therapy or counselling sessions and many are very sceptical about the benefits of talking things through with someone who, at least initially, is a complete stranger. However, there is no doubt that one of the most effective and long-lasting treatments for an eating disorder is some form of therapy or counselling, coupled with careful attention to medical and nutritional needs. Ideally, this treatment should be tailored to the individual and will vary according to both the severity of the disorder and the patient's individual problems, needs and strengths. This chapter provides an overview of some of the types of therapy available to young people suffering from an eating disorder.

The general aims of therapy for a young person with an eating disorder are to:

- explore the thoughts and feelings that led to the eating disorder

- help the patient overcome his obsession with body shape and size

- help the patient overcome his fears about eating

- help the patient improve his self-esteem

- help the patient establish a healthy approach to eating that will ensure an appropriate level of weight gain.

As well as one-to-one counselling and psychotherapy, many therapies are used in the treatment of eating disorders. The main ones include:

- group therapy

- occupational therapy which might include art, music and drama therapy

- family therapy

- cognitive behavioural therapy.

Group therapy

Many young children and teenagers find individual therapy so daunting that they just clam up. They see the therapist as yet another adult who doesn't understand them and who is trying to make them do something they do not want to do. Certainly Joe fitted into this group. He couldn't really communicate with his keyworker (psychotherapist) on a one-to-one basis. He liked her, but he felt he was well on the way to getting better simply by being at the in-patient unit and he didn't feel comfortable discussing personal issues with her. Instead he would pour out all his troubles to me and then I would try to relay them back to his keyworker.

In contrast he found the group therapy sessions at the unit much easier to deal with. Some of the sessions encouraged the patients to speak about their difficulties. Even when Joe didn't join in he derived some benefit from hearing about how the other patients were feeling. Other sessions were more structured with role-plays and problem-solving tasks. Joe found these sessions useful, easy to participate in and he even enjoyed some of them.

Many patients feel safe in group therapy sessions. They are with people experiencing similar problems and feelings. They can join in if they feel like it or be passive observers if they don't. Many patients have been suffering from feelings of isolation and low self-esteem for some time. They soon realise that other patients in the group feel the same way. In a successful group the patients will stop looking just to the therapist for support and they will start to give each other support.

To participate in a group session the patient needs to be able to overcome any fear he may have of interacting socially. This is important as many anorexics lack assertiveness. Group discussions enable the patients to re-evaluate their attitudes to shape and body weight through other people's eyes. This can help them to realise how illogical and irrational their thought processes have become. As a patient becomes bolder and more confident he can make a positive contribution to group discussions and start to question his fear of food and becoming fat.

Occupational therapy

This is really another form of group therapy and may include art, music and drama therapy. Patients are encouraged to express themselves through drawing, painting and sculpture, music or a variety of drama activities. Their work is assessed and evaluated by therapists specialising in this form of treatment. Patients often find these types of therapy very relaxing, as well as being useful ways of exploring underlying emotions.

Family therapy

Most professionals in the field of eating disorders in young people will agree that family therapy is one of the most important ways of treating the disease. Family therapists are trained to help the members of the family unit to:

- talk to each other about the patient's illness

- discuss the effects it is having on the individual members of the family

- discuss the effects it is having on relationships within the family

- identify things which might need discussion and resolution

- consider any actions that might help improve things for the patient and his family in the home environment.

Depending on the stage of the patient's illness the family might be asked to try and take responsibility for feeding their child, or at least to take a central role in supporting their child's efforts to eat. Ideas about how to improve things might flow easily from the discussion, although not many families find family therapy easy. The therapist might have to take a pro-active role in encouraging all the members of the family to speak up. Certainly in our first session Joe only spoke when spoken to and then his answers were monosyllabic. His younger brother Tom, who was only nine years old at the time, spent the entire session drawing pictures and basically ignored the therapist when she tried to speak to him. Subsequent sessions were easier and we all got more out of them. When Joe was discharged from the in-patient unit we changed to a different family therapist. We all found her much easier to talk to, but this may simply have been a function of the fact that Joe was well on his way to recovery and we were all more relaxed. However, if you find that you are not making much progress with one therapist it is worth trying to find another as your family may simply get on better with someone who takes a slightly different approach or has a slightly different character.

Many families feel defensive when they are asked to attend family therapy. They feel that they are being blamed for their child's illness. Some families even refuse to attend on the grounds that their other children are fine and so there cannot be anything wrong with the family set-up. It is important to remember that nobody is trying to blame the family, everyone is trying to help the anorexic child recover. The family knows their child best and in family therapy it is the family who can help the therapist by highlighting important issues. As parents you are important allies both to your son and the medical team. Family therapy can put you in a stronger position to help your son conquer his illness and get through the recovery phase.

Cognitive behavioural therapy (CBT)

CBT treats emotional disorders by changing negative patterns of thought. It is now well established as a key method of helping overcome psychologically based disorders such as anorexia nervosa. Unlike other therapies CBT is very scientific and its approach suits many anorexics for two reasons:

1. CBT is very structured and very logical. This often suits anorexics who like a strict routine and to feel that they are in control.

2. CBT does not try to delve in to the past. Again this suits many anorexics who either feel unable, or unwilling, to address upsetting issues from their past life.

In CBT the patient and therapist will work together to identify problem areas such as the patient's belief that he is fat and stupid. His belief that he is fat and stupid is likely to make him feel low in mood and to withdraw socially. As he becomes more and more withdrawn there is no one to challenge his negative beliefs even if they are not at all true and in reality he is very thin and very clever. It is a vicious circle which, over time, lowers the patients self-esteem and leads the patient to seek more and more comfort from his anorexia. In addition negative thoughts tend to lead to negative feelings, which in turn lead to negative behaviour. Here are three examples:

1. Negative thought: Eating will make me fat.
   Negative feeling: I am scared of getting fat.
   Negative behaviour: I will not eat for the rest of the day.

2. Negative thought: I must exercise constantly to keep thin.
   Negative feeling: I am scared of putting on weight if I don't exercise.
   Negative behaviour: I must exercise as much as possible.

3. Negative thought: I am useless at maths.
   Negative feeling: I will look stupid if I answer a question in class.
   Negative behaviour: If I don't join in, in class I will not look stupid.

Once the therapist has built up a trusting relationship with his patient he will start to challenge his beliefs, anxieties and any negative thoughts. He will also encourage the patient to keep a diary of his thoughts and moods in response to day-to-day situations. Initially many of the patient's automatic thoughts will be negative. Over time the therapist will help the patient learn to challenge his negative thoughts and to replace them with positive thoughts. The patient will start to identify which of his thoughts are illogical and irrational. This may take some time, but eventually the patient will start to accept that he is not fat, he needs to eat a balanced diet to be healthy, he needs to exercise in moderation to be healthy and in reality he is quite good at maths.

For Joe a key example of how he challenged his negative thoughts relating to putting on weight was:

- Situation: The re-feeding programme was making Joe put on weight.

- Emotion: Fear and panic over getting too fat.

- Automatic negative thought: I'm going to be too fat to be in the school football team.

- Positive thought: I have been very ill and was too thin and weak to do any sport. I need to put on weight to be strong enough to be in the football team. I need to put on the weight gradually and then to eat a healthy diet to ensure I keep growing. I need to eat enough to build up strength to be able to play a whole football match.

Whilst CBT does not suit everyone it has been found to be particularly useful for treating anorexics. Joe found the logic and structure much easier to deal with than the vague exploratory nature of individual psychotherapy. It also helped that Joe's CB therapist was a sporty young man who Joe could relate to and didn't feel threatened by. Therapy is such an individual thing and there is very much an element of trial and error in finding the right therapist and the right therapies for each individual case.

Other approaches

There are also many other therapies available if your son finds he is not suited to the ones mentioned above. For example, the National Institute of Clinical Excellence (NICE) published guidelines in January 2004 which advocated several psychological treatments which have been successfully adapted for anorexia nervosa including:

- **Cognitive analytic therapy (CAT)**. This is a psychological treatment in which a therapist works with a person to help them to make positive changes in their lives and to build a future. This can require understanding what has prevented them from making changes in the past and improving the way they cope with problems. CAT is 'analytic' in the sense that it explores unconscious motivations.

- **Interpersonal therapy (IPT)**. This is a specific form of psychotherapy that is designed to help patients identify and address current interpersonal problems. In this treatment there is no emphasis on directly modifying eating habits; rather, it is expected that they will change as interpersonal functioning improves.

- **Focal psychodynamic therapy**. This therapy works at identifying and focusing on a central conflict or difficulty in a person's early life that is having an impact on that person's current problems.

There is also the enormous field of alternative or complementary therapies, which you might want to try one or more of. We tried magnetic field therapy with Joe, although it didn't really suit him. Complementary therapies can be expensive, but some are available on the NHS. It is important to check whether your therapist is properly qualified before proceeding with complementary therapy. Examples of complementary therapies often used to tackle emotional problems and to aid relaxation include:

- acupuncture
- hypnotherapy
- reflexology
- yoga
- aromatherapy.

There is no doubt that therapy is a crucial part of an anorexic's treatment programme. As you can see there are many choices, but your son's medical team should be well qualified to come up with a suitable programme for him. Therapy is difficult. You are trying to address extremely complex emotional feelings. There is no magic cure, but if you find the right therapy programme for your son he will have made a big step towards recovery.

10. Healthy eating

One of the most difficult things for recovering anorexics is to establish a healthy eating regime. Teenage boys need more calories per day to maintain a healthy growth pattern than an adult male who works in an office. For most people the term 'healthy eating' conjures up images of grilled meat and fish with piles of salad, vegetables and fruit. Teenage boys and indeed girls need more than that to meet their dietary needs. Lots of carbohydrate, even in the form of junk food, is a necessary part of a teenager's diet, as well as a reasonable amount of sweets and puddings. This chapter provides some practical tips on how to:

- help an anorexic teenage boy put weight on

- ensure that a 'recovered' anorexic doesn't slide back down the slippery slope, simply because he or his carer has failed to recognise how much an active teenage boy needs to eat to maintain a healthy growth pattern

- ensure through this process that a healthy balanced diet is consumed.

At school children are taught at an early age about the different food groups and that a balanced diet must contain:

- proteins for growth and tissue repair

- carbohydrates for energy

- fats to store energy and provide warmth

- vitamins for good health

- minerals for good health

- fibre to prevent constipation

- water to keep the body hydrated.

They learn why they need these different food groups, which foods provide good sources of these groups and the importance of eating a balanced diet which provides everything that is required for healthy growth, repair of damaged cells and enough energy for the body's activities.

Anorexics very quickly forget everything they have learnt about healthy eating. Many become preoccupied with the calorific values of everything they eat and they quickly learn which foods to avoid in order to achieve the maximum weight loss. Others are less scientific. They simply eliminate certain foods from their diet, which they fear will make them fat. The end result is the same. A very restrictive diet which lacks many of the vitamins and minerals needed to maintain good health and one which includes plenty of fruit and vegetables, a reasonable amount of protein, but very little in the way of carbohydrates and fat.

The problems for anorexics returning to healthy eating are huge and shouldn't be underestimated. Consider the following issues facing an active anorexic teenage boy:

- He must completely rethink his approach to food and overcome his enormous fear that certain food types will make him fat.

- In order to return to a more normal weight he must eat even more than his peers do and almost certainly more than anyone else in the rest of the family must.

- Undoubtedly his stomach will have shrunk and to start with, eating more food will make him feel extremely uncomfortable. He may even experience quite severe stomach pains at the beginning.

- Once he has achieved a reasonable weight he must learn how much to eat to maintain a healthy growth pattern.

- In doing this he must learn to balance his food intake with his physical activity and many anorexic teenagers are very active.

When Joe first came home to visit from the in-patient unit, he was still on his re-feeding programme. I was given very clear guidance for his meals and I soon learned how to boost the calorie count of a meal by adding butter or cream. He had to eat a lot of very rich food to ensure he consumed enough calories to gain weight. When he reached his target weight I was amazed how much food he had to continue to eat to maintain a reasonable growth pattern. Both Joe and I were nervous to start with but we muddled through and managed to find the right diet for Joe. When he was discharged from the in-patient unit he had reached his target weight, but was then told his target had been moved up by 2 kg because he was three months older than when the first target was set and he had grown taller. We faced the challenge of making sure he continued to gain weight or he would have to go back to the unit. Eating at home is never as easy as eating in a specialist unit where the staff are trained to deal with all types of eating disorder. In the unit Joe had no choice. At home he felt he could argue and negotiate when it came to food. I had to be very firm, but also let him start to take some responsibility for his eating. If he resisted one type of food I backed off for a while and made up for it by introducing a different food. Over time Joe stopped being fearful of dairy products like cheese and cream and he now eats a very well-balanced diet and lots of it.

As I have already explained, Joe was an in-patient in a specialist unit while going through his re-feeding programme and his diet was carefully worked out by a dietician. Of course it is possible to introduce a re-feeding programme or diet plan in the home, but it is an enormous challenge and it is worth considering the following issues:

- You cannot force a child to eat. You must work with him, give him lots of support and encouragement and he must want to get better.

- Sometimes it helps to have the endorsement of someone outside the immediate family that the child respects. This might your GP, a favourite teacher or even someone in the wider family such as a sporty uncle.

- The earlier you start the better. A child who has only been restricting his food for a short period of time will find it much easier to reverse these habits than one who cannot remember a time when he didn't have a fear of many food types. Similarly a child who has only lost 10% of his body weight will find it much easier to regain that weight than a child who has lost 25% of his body weight and has become irrational through a long period of malnourishment.

- The basic aim is to increase the sufferer's daily calorie intake so that he starts to gain weight. At the same time it is important to make sure that his diet is well-balanced. As long as the carer has a good knowledge of the calorific value of food and a good idea of what constitutes a balanced diet, then it should be possible to put together a perfectly good diet plan both for weight gain and for maintenance of healthy growth once a reasonable weight has been achieved.

- If you are fortunate enough to have access to a dietician, perhaps through your local health centre, then it makes sense to seek his/her advice in putting together a diet plan.

- Sometimes it is impossible to persuade an anorexic to adopt a diet plan at home. If you try and fail you will be joining many other families who have gone through the same experience. Joe was very ill by the time his anorexia was diagnosed and we needed professional help to get him back on his feet. Never be afraid or embarrassed to go to your GP and ask for specialist help.

Once Joe was back on his feet and back home I needed to make sure that he maintained a healthy and balanced diet that would ensure he continued to grow. I found the food pyramid a useful way of ensuring that Joe's diet included a good balance of all the food groups. It was also a useful way of explaining to Joe why he had to eat certain types of food he wasn't too keen on. The food pyramid is an outline of what to eat each day based on US government dietary guidelines. It was developed by the US Department of Agriculture (USDA) and has been widely adopted by organisations interested in food and nutrition. The concept is simple. You eat more of the foods at the bottom of the pyramid and less of each category as you move up. The USDA also provides guidance on the appropriate size of each serving. The advice from the USDA is to eat at least the lowest number of recommended servings from the five major food groups listed below. You need them for the vitamins, minerals, carbohydrates and protein they provide. The USDA website can be found at www.nal.usda.gov

The Food Guide Pyramid

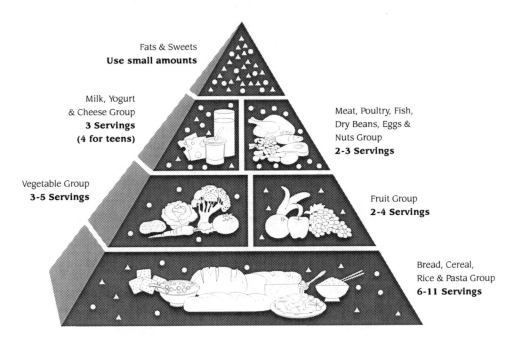

Source: U.S. Department of Agriculture and the U.S. Department of Health and Human Services

The food pyramid categories

- Carbohydrates make up the bottom layer of the pyramid. These include bread, cereals, rice and pasta. It is recommended that you eat between six and eleven servings. Examples of a serving are one slice of bread, one ounce of ready-to-eat cereal, half a cup of cooked cereal, rice or pasta.

- Fruit and vegetables make up the next layer. It is recommended that you eat between two and four servings of fruit and between three and five servings of vegetables. Examples of a serving of fruit are one medium apple, banana or orange, half a cup of chopped, cooked, or canned fruit, three quarters of a cup of fruit juice. Examples of a serving of vegetables are one cup of raw leafy vegetables, half a cup of other vegetables, cooked or chopped raw, or three quarters of a cup of vegetable juice.

- The third layer is made up of proteins. There are two groups of equal importance. It is recommended that you eat three servings of the milk, yoghurt and cheese group and two to three servings of the meat, poultry, fish, eggs, beans and nuts group. Examples of a serving are one cup of milk or yoghurt, one and a half ounces of natural cheese, two ounces of processed cheese, two to three ounces of cooked lean meat, poultry, or fish, half a cup of cooked dry beans. One egg or two tablespoons of peanut butter count as one ounce of lean meat. It is important to trim fat off meat to stay within the guidelines.

- The top layer is made up of fats, oils and sweets. No specific serving size is given for the fats, oils, and sweets group because the message is use sparingly. However, this is still an important part of your diet and recovering anorexics should be guided to eat these in moderation. It is likely that during his illness, an anorexic boy will have excluded this group altogether.

A diet plan based on the food pyramid should provide all the nutrients, vitamins, minerals, carbohydrates and protein that a growing child needs. Anorexics are likely to be deficient in certain areas to start with and so it is important to ensure there is enough:

- protein to replace wasted muscle and encourage growth

- calcium to strengthen bones that may have been weakened through a prolonged period of starvation

- iron, as many anorexics are anaemic.

If in doubt consult your doctor or a dietician.

Once a diet plan has been established the next challenge is to put it into action. There are some important things to note when trying to introduce a new eating regime for an anorexic boy:

- Every individual's calorie requirement is different and there is an element of trial and error in working out how many calories each boy needs to consume in order to gain and then to maintain his weight. As a general guide most teenagers need to consume between 1,500 and 2,500 calories a day to maintain their weight. A very active teenage boy is likely to be at the upper end of this range and some boys may need even more than this. To gain weight he will need more. An extra 1,000 calories a day is likely to lead to a weekly weight gain of around 1 kg, although again each boy will be different. Therefore a very active anorexic teenage boy may need to consume as much as 3,500 to 4,000 calories a day to gain a reasonable amount of weight.

- Build up the calories gradually. If a boy has been eating 1,000 calories a day for some time, it is unrealistic to expect him to suddenly jump to 3,000 or more in one step. Indeed it can be dangerous for a severely under nourished child to increase his food intake too quickly as it can put pressure on an already weakened heart. Try introducing a few hundred extra calories each day. If he struggles stay at the same level for a few days and then try increasing again. Taking a slow gentle approach in which the sufferer gradually gets used to eating more food is more likely to work than a fast track approach. The sufferer is likely to need lots of support and encouragement as he increases his food intake.

- To start with try to introduce foods that are gentle on the stomach. Milky drinks, yoghurt and honey and light desserts are a good way of adding calories without putting too much strain on a shrunken and sensitive stomach. If your son complains of stomach pains for more than a few days he should see a doctor.

- Anorexics tend to have a real fear of certain foods. Common examples include chocolate, chips, cheese and cream. Introduce them slowly, one at a time. If the sufferer refuses one food try to make up for it in different ways and then try again at a later stage. Explain that eating the occasional Mars bar, a bag of chips or a cheese sandwich is only going to slightly increase their total calorie intake for that day. It is not going to automatically make them gain a kg.

- Junk food has its place in a teenager's diet. It provides carbohydrate and lots of energy. Obviously a teenager shouldn't just eat junk food and those who do tend to be sickly and obese. Junk food in moderation is a useful way of providing extra calories and energy and most teenagers enjoy the occasional pizza, burger and chips, crisps, chocolate, sweets and cakes.

- Ready meals can have their place in a balanced diet. The calorific values are clearly stated, they are quick to prepare and teenagers often like them. In addition, the calories in ready meals can easily be boosted by adding extra cream to sauces, adding extra rice, potatoes or pasta and so on.

- Gaining weight is an incredibly stressful experience for an anorexic. Only weigh him once a week. Sometimes it is helpful for the sufferer if he doesn't see the scales. If you are not sure what weight your son should be contact your health visitor or GP who will be able to advise you.

- Once the sufferer has reached a reasonable weight his diet must be adjusted to ensure he doesn't gain too much weight. Try reducing his daily consumption by between 500 and 1,000 calories, and monitor his weight for several more weeks. Adjust his calorie intake as necessary to maintain his weight at a reasonable level. As the weeks go by you will find the appropriate food intake by trial and error. As the months go by the sufferer will start to be able to take some responsibility for his own food intake. Eventually he will be able to respond to his own appetite without having to really think about it.

- Learning how much to eat and how to eat healthily are huge challenges for an anorexic. There are bound to be setbacks. Some may be minor, others may be major. When they happen take a deep breath and start again. The sufferer will need lots and lots of love, support and encouragement if he is to get through in one piece.

With Joe I wasn't obsessive about the number of calories he was consuming, but we worked out an appropriate diet through trial and error. He had to eat a huge amount to maintain a healthy growth pattern. Six months after he was discharged from the specialist unit I felt I could let him have more responsibility for his own diet and I stopped watching his every move. I still kept a close eye on his attitude to food and at times he needed encouragement to have proper meals, particularly in the school holidays. A year after he was discharged I felt I could totally relax. Even if he skipped a meal in the holidays I knew he would make up for it by snacking on the move, which is something that most normal teenagers do. Now, three years later, he is still very active but we don't have to consciously watch what he is eating. His appetite is huge and it now tells him when to eat, not the anorexia!

11. Caring for the carer

There is no doubt that caring for an anorexic child is an incredibly stressful experience. Caring for any sick child is stressful, but in most cases the sick child wants to get better and will happily go along with the appropriate treatment programme. On the other hand anorexia is a mental illness and it is one where diagnosis is difficult and denial is a common feature. The child might refuse to accept there is anything wrong. Even if he does accept he is ill he may have no desire to get better. In fact the idea of putting on weight and eating normal meals probably petrifies him and faced with this prospect he can be extremely difficult and irrational. The rest of the family is all affected in some way. The stress of dealing with this scenario can be compared to:

- looking after a child with cancer: you have no idea how long treatment will take or whether your child will make a full recovery

- looking after a family member with schizophrenia, whose behaviour is totally unpredictable and can be violent

- looking after a family member with Alzheimer's, whose behaviour is totally unpredictable and can be harmful to the very confused patient.

It is important that the carer(s) finds ways of coping with this stress, because if the carer(s) breaks under the strain the son is almost certain to succumb to the anorexia and the anorexia is likely to take control of the whole family. Everyone reacts to stress differently and will have his or her own ways of dealing with that stress. In this chapter, I mention some of the things that we found useful including:

- the benefits of support groups and helplines

- using your GP, health visitor or a counsellor

- the importance of close friends/family

- the importance of the carer(s) keeping some time to relax or to pursue a hobby away from the anorexic boy.

Support groups

In Chapter 7, I gave details of the services provided by the Eating Disorder Association. The EDA website contains a list of support groups run by volunteers. Many of these groups offer support to carers as well as to the sufferers. There may also be other carer support groups in your local area, which you might discover through your local volunteer bureau, your health centre, your local hospital, your library, your local newspaper, the Citizens Advice Bureau or by searching on the Internet.

We joined the parents/carers' group at Joe's in-patient unit. It met once a month and included some time when the nursing staff were available to answer any questions. Then we were left to chat among ourselves. Joe's unit included children with a wide range of behavioural problems so we spoke to parents who were dealing with different illnesses. However, this didn't really matter. At the end of the day we were all in the same boat trying to deal with a child who was having difficulty coping with normal life. We could share our experiences and talk about the stresses and strains of caring for such a child, the feelings of despair when being faced with another setback or yet another tantrum. We could also talk about our own coping strategies and share practical tips for dealing with what often seemed to be impossible situations. Most importantly we could talk about recovery and hope for the future. Several of the parents were looking forward to their child being discharged and we talked about strategies for the recovery phase and reintegration back into the home environment.

Support groups come in many forms. If you are lucky enough to have one in your local area, you have nothing to lose by attending a meeting. It might not suit you, but if it does then it can provide much needed comfort and support when you are feeling overwhelmed by the challenges ahead.

Helplines

The EDA helpline provides you with the opportunity to talk to others who have gone through similar experiences. The main helpline number is 0845 634 1414. There is also a team of volunteer phone contacts, email contacts and postal contacts who you can contact if you wish to have a continuing dialogue with one person.

There is also a national carer's line, which operates from Wednesday to Friday. They can send you an information pack or you can talk directly to someone who will give you general advice and information on being a carer. It is not a listening service as such but can give you advice about benefits available for carers. You can call free on 0808 808 7777.

If you are feeling really desperate the Samaritans are always there to offer support to anyone facing an emotional crisis. Sometimes you feel so low that you cannot bear to talk to anyone in your close family or social circle. A call to the Samaritans can help relieve the immediate pressure. Call 08457 909090.

Your GP, health visitor or counsellor

The stress of looking after an anorexic child can have a detrimental impact on your health. Signs of stress include:

- headaches
- racing heart
- clammy hands
- sweating
- loss of appetite
- nausea
- insomnia
- tiredness
- increased drinking/ smoking
- lack of concentration
- feelings of helplessness and failure
- depression and anxiety
- crying.

Your GP or health visitor might be able to help you deal with this increased stress, perhaps using relaxation techniques. If you feel your GP is not being sympathetic you might consider seeing a different GP. You might also consider seeing a trained counsellor who is used to dealing with people facing very stressful periods in their lives. Again, you might need to try a couple of different counsellors before you find one who suits your needs.

Some people find that alternative therapies suit them better to help them cope with the added stress. It doesn't do any harm to try one or two to see if they help your individual situation.

Close family and friends

A problem shared is a problem halved. Not everyone in your family and not all your close friends will be good at giving you support, but they may be able to help in other ways. I found it useful to mentally categorise my family and friends into the following groups:

- Soul mates. Those who would be happy to listen patiently as I and/or my husband poured our hearts out over the latest setback or trauma and who would make comforting and soothing comments. They would also be happy to challenge any irrational thoughts we might be having about Joe's progress, his treatment programme and so on.

- Practical helpers. Those who would step in at a minute's notice to help with Joe or the rest of the family. They would provide a much-needed break for me and/or my husband to escape for a few hours.

- Social distractions. Those who would drag my husband and I out to play golf, go to the cinema or have a meal and try to forget about the traumas of Joe even for a few hours.

- Need to know. Family members or friends who found it difficult to cope with or comprehend the issues we were facing and dealing with on a daily basis. We kept these people informed on a minimal need to know basis.

For me, my husband was included in all of the first three categories. We were also very lucky to have a very close-knit circle of family and friends who were happy to help in any way that they could. If you are not in such a fortunate position it is even more important to consider joining some sort of carer's support group or to seek out a trained counsellor who could help you through these difficult times.

Relaxation and hobbies

It is very easy to become so wrapped up in your son's illness that you forget to take time out for relaxation and hobbies. We all have different ways of relaxing and relieving the day-to-day stresses of life. It is important for you as a carer to remember to give yourself time to relax and escape from your son's illness on a regular basis. To start with I wasn't very good at giving myself time out. I became stressed, lay awake at night and lost weight. As time went on and I came to accept Joe's illness and its effect on our family, I realised how important it was for everyone to have time out from Joe's illness. I found writing, exercise, golf and going out with friends every now and then were very therapeutic. There are lots of activities that it might be useful to consider including:

- Music – listening to it, singing along with it, dancing to it, playing an instrument.

- Reading – preferably not the latest book on eating disorders, but something that will distract you for a few hours.

- Writing – a diary of your experiences, some poetry, a short story or memoirs from your childhood. Anything that you find therapeutic.

- Exercise – of any kind. I prefer outdoor exercise, you might prefer going to the gym or to an aerobics or yoga class.

- Personal pampering – don't forget to have your hair cut. You also might consider a massage, pedicure, manicure or other soothing treatment.

- Shopping – either on your own or with the rest of the family. Perhaps treat yourselves to something you might not normally consider buying.

- Short breaks or days out – there are lots of really good value short breaks on offer, which might help distract you and the rest of your family from the stresses and strains of living with anorexia.

- Personal space at home – this is one of the most important things to consider. As a carer of an anorexic child you are constantly dealing with high levels of stress. Make sure you have somewhere to escape to even for a few minutes to cool off after the latest tantrum. Having a relaxing bath with the bathroom door firmly locked or escaping with a good book to the end of the garden are practical examples of finding space at home.

There is no doubt that caring for an anorexic child is extremely stressful. If the carer makes no time to look after him/herself then he/she is likely to crack under the strain and the anorexia will take over the whole family. The stress can be reduced enormously by making good use of the support network around you and by giving yourself quality time out from your anorexic child.

12. Returning to normal life

Your son has reached a reasonable weight, his mood has lifted, he has started seeing his friends again and is back at school. He is still seeing his psychiatrist, but only every few months to make sure there are no signs of relapse. Everyone in the family can breathe a huge sigh of relief and look forward to returning to a normal life.

Unfortunately it is not quite as simple as that. The process of recovery from anorexia is very complex and often quite lengthy. It's a little like learning to drive. You have an intense period of driving lessons, you learn the highway code inside out, you know that lots of people fail their test at the first attempt and you are delighted when you pass at the second attempt. However, you don't really learn to drive properly until you are out on the road on your own. The driving lessons and the test have prepared you for many eventualities, but once you are out on the road on your own you suddenly find yourself being faced with many different situations that you haven't seen before. You have to use your common sense and instinct to know how to react. Occasionally you might make a mistake, but within a year of driving on your own you are likely to be a much more competent driver.

Recovering from anorexia can be a similar process. Each case is different and every family is different so there is no magic formula to tell you how to return to normal life. Mistakes can be made and relapse rates are fairly high, but if the family works together and is aware of what to look out for, then the chances of recurrence can be minimised and the family can look forward to a normal life.

Relapse can happen for a variety of reasons. Consider the following scenarios:

1. Peter has been a model in-patient whilst on his re-feeding programme and whilst going through therapy. However, deep down he is still very much controlled by his anorexia. His main aim is to get away from all the doctors who he really despises. Once he reaches a reasonable weight and is discharged from his in-patient unit he very quickly reverts to his anorexic ways and his weight starts to fall off again. He goes back to the in-patient unit, puts on weight and comes home again after a few months. He maintains his weight for slightly longer this time, but then loses his place in the school football team. This triggers another relapse and he loses a huge amount of weight very quickly. His third stay at the in-patient unit is much longer. He finds a therapist who he

trusts and this really helps him. For the first time he really genuinely wants to beat his illness.

2. Paul has struggled with anorexia for several years. He has never been ill enough to warrant an in-patient admission, but he has been undergoing therapy and re-feeding as a day-patient for six months. He feels very secure at the day centre. He finds it easy to eat the food there and derives much support from being with other recovering anorexics. He enjoys his therapy sessions and has a particularly good relationship with his keyworker. He genuinely wants to beat his anorexia. Unfortunately when he is discharged from the day centre he quickly loses his ability to fight off the anorexic thoughts which still lurk in his head. He feels lost. He finds it hard to eat school dinners, which are very different from the ones he had at the day centre. He starts to get anxious about how much he is eating at home and starts to cut down. Within a few months of discharge he starts losing weight again. He feels depressed but cannot fight off the anorexic voice in his head. He returns to the day centre for several months. His keyworker helps him to overcome his anxieties about eating in other situations such as at school, at home or out socially. Next time he is discharged he feels much stronger and is able to maintain his weight.

These are two very different situations. In the first scenario Peter has no intention of getting better. He is playing the system to get home as quickly as possible. At one stage some of Joe's medical team felt that he was doing exactly this as he was such a model patient to start with, but thankfully this wasn't the case and Joe genuinely wanted to get better. In Peter's situation there is very little that anyone could do. An anorexic will rarely get better just by putting on weight. He must genuinely want to get better and even then will need lots of support from everyone around him in order to achieve this. Having found a therapist he trusts is a big step in the right direction but he still has a long way to go.

In the second scenario Paul genuinely wants to get better but feels vulnerable once he is released from the security of the day centre. His relapse might have been avoided if he and his family had been better prepared for his homecoming. The issue of school meals is very often a difficult one for recovering anorexics and an area that they need considerable support with for some time. Some school canteens can provide special meals to start with, which are similar to those that the anorexic has been used to in his recovery phase. Sometimes it helps if a best friend or favourite teacher can provide encouragement during school mealtimes. Mealtimes at home can be equally difficult if no special arrangements are made. If a sufferer returns home to find exactly the same family eating patterns as when he started his treatment programme he might naturally slip into his old anorexic ways. Careful planning can help to avoid this. A small change in a family's eating routine can make a big difference. Your son is likely to feel anxious about being discharged from the security of his treatment regime. It is important to try to make this transition as easy as possible for him and to take into account that he is still likely to be anxious about food and weight for some time to come.

Relapse can be triggered by many things, but there are certain situations and events which are more likely to trigger a relapse and in which your son might need extra support to help avoid a relapse. These include:

- **Holidays**. Your son might just have got used to a more normal diet at home when the whole family goes off on holiday. Eating patterns tend to be different in a holiday situation. The food might be very different from the food at home especially if you go somewhere exotic. In addition people generally eat much more on holiday than they do at home. This whole situation may petrify your son. He is not sure how much to eat to maintain his weight. He certainly doesn't want to put too much weight on, but feels pressurised by everyone eating more than usual around him. It might be appropriate to discuss these issues with your son before going on holiday, and to devise a food plan that he is happy with and that it is easy for him to adhere to without ruining his holiday.

- **An emotional setback**. This could be a major event such as the death of a favourite grandparent or an apparently minor event such as not getting the part he wants in the school play. It could be losing a place in the sports team or splitting up from a girlfriend. There are many situations that can cause an emotional setback. Hopefully your son will feel better able to deal with such setbacks post-anorexia, but there may be times when he is especially vulnerable. It is important to encourage your son to talk about things that are upsetting him. He may not always feel like talking to you about all of his issues, and in some cases he might find it easier to talk to a friend or favourite relative. In any event it is a good idea to watch out for your son suddenly becoming more withdrawn and/or suffering from uncharacteristic mood swings.

Another thing that some families find difficult is that their son's character post-anorexia seems very different from his character pre-anorexia. This is not necessarily a bad thing, in fact it is normally a very positive thing, but it can take some getting used to. Young people who develop anorexia are often model children. They work hard at school and are easy to live with at home.

Post-anorexia they can seem to be much more demanding and assertive. They have had to develop these characteristics to beat their anorexia and their new found confidence, self-esteem and assertiveness will make them much more well equipped to deal with life's ups and downs in the future. Joe was a very easy child pre-anorexia. He rarely complained and did well in all aspects of his school life. Post-anorexia he is much more likely to stand up for himself and to complain if he feels hard done by. He is also much more likely to let me know if something is upsetting him emotionally. He is simply a stronger person all round having gone through the experience of anorexia. A very positive outcome of his experience at the in-patient unit is that he has become very supportive of people who he feels are disadvantaged in some way. This might be a younger boy at school, a disabled person in the street or a charity that catches his eye.

Thus far I have given some health warnings about returning to normal life post-anorexia. It is better to be on the look out for signs of a relapse than to be blissfully unaware as anorexia tries to creep back into your son's life. Whilst it is never an easy road to travel, many anorexics do make a full recovery and go on to lead a completely normal life. In turn their families can return to a normal life although it is likely that some changes to the family routine will have been made along the way. Other anorexics never fully recover but learn to live with their illness. In turn their families adapt to make life as easy as possible for all family members and to give as much support as they can to the sufferer. Their lives may never completely return to normal but they learn to live with the anorexia in as harmonious way as possible.

Anorexia is a terrifying experience for any family to go through, but remember:

- Boys can get anorexia too.

- Anorexia can be beaten.

- The sooner anorexia is confronted the more chance there is of a full recovery.

- Don't leave it too long before seeking professional help.

- Try to let the anorexic recover at his own pace.

- Look forward not back.

- Never give up hope.

And most importantly, you are not alone.

13. Do boys get other eating disorders?

The simple answer is yes. Anorexia is one of a range of eating disorders and boys are certainly prone to suffer from any of them. Whilst the different illnesses have different symptoms and effects, many of the approaches to self-help and treatment will be similar to those used for anorexics. At the end of the day the main aim for anyone suffering from an eating disorder is to re-establish healthy eating patterns, maintain a healthy weight and to regain self-confidence and self-esteem. Much of what is written in the self-help and treatment options section of this book should be useful for the carer of a boy suffering from one of these other eating disorders. I also recommend reading *Fit to Die* by Anna Paterson, published in 2004 by Lucky Duck Publishing. In this book the author draws the reader's attention to the characteristics of and special difficulties for men with eating disorders.

Other eating disorders include bulimia nervosa, binge eating, compulsive exercising and 'ED-NOS' (eating disorders not otherwise specified). This chapter contains a brief description of each illness, what to look out for and the effects of the illness.

Bulimia nervosa

The term bulimia nervosa literally means 'the hunger of an ox'. It is only since the 1970s that it has been recognised by the medical community. Sufferers are caught in a cycle of eating huge quantities of food (binge eating) and then getting rid of that food by vomiting, taking laxatives and diuretics, excessive exercising or a combination of any of these. It is thought that male sufferers are more likely to exercise excessively to get rid of the calories, whilst female sufferers are more likely to vomit.

Sufferers often eat very quickly, almost in a panic, and their eating is out of control. They feel incredibly guilty after each binge, which is why they will then purge. Like anorexics they have a fear of being fat, are often deeply unhappy about some aspect of their life and have low self-esteem. Despite this they are often high achievers and from the outside can appear to be outgoing and self-assured. Unlike anorexics, sufferers of bulimia often have a normal body weight and this feature means it is very difficult to detect the illness. People with bulimia tend not to seek help or support very readily.

It is thought that bulimia is more common than anorexia, but because it is such a hidden illness it is difficult to come up with accurate figures. It tends to develop at a later age than anorexia and rarely before late teens. However with all the cultural pressures for boys to be fit and slim it is possible that younger boys will start to develop the illness at an earlier age in order to achieve the perfect size and shape. Bulimics may go on to develop anorexia. Many anorexics also have episodes of bulimia.

These are some of the things to look out for if you suspect that your son might be suffering from bulimia nervosa:

- an unhealthy interest in food and regular binges which seem out of control

- an obsession with exercise particularly after eating a large meal or bingeing

- an obsession with achieving a particular body weight or physique

- an intense fear of becoming fat

- frequent weight changes

- food disappearing from the kitchen in large amounts

- food being hoarded in the bedroom

- disappearing to the toilet straight after each meal or binge to vomit

- evidence in the bathroom that someone has recently vomited

- complaints of sore throat which can be caused by vomiting

- an increase in tooth decay which can be caused by stomach acid in the mouth

- complaints of stomach pains and/or constipation

- vomiting can cause salivary glands to swell giving a much rounder appearance to the face, which is not accompanied by general weight gain

- deterioration in skin condition

- an unexplained increase in lethargy and tiredness

- an increase in mood swings and irrational behaviour

- evidence of low self-esteem and depression

- withdrawal from normal social circle and becoming more isolated at home.

As with any eating disorder it is worth noting down any changes you notice in your son's behaviour. This will help your GP to diagnose the illness if it gets to the stage where you feel you need to seek professional medical help. Bulimia is a very dangerous illness and if you suspect your son is suffering from it you should seek medical help as soon as possible.

Not only are there the obvious problems caused by regular vomiting and laxative abuse, there are also several hidden dangers. The binge and purge cycle can cause an imbalance in, or lead to dangerously low levels of, the essential minerals in the body. Very low levels of potassium are common in bulimics. This in turn can significantly or fatally affect the workings of the vital internal organs. Dramatic changes to weight can also put a huge amount of pressure on the heart.

If your GP diagnoses bulimia it is likely that your son will then be immediately referred on to a specialist in eating disorders. Treatment is likely to be a combination of introducing a structured and healthy eating pattern and some sort of therapy to seek to resolve any underlying emotional problems. Re-educating the body is not easy and there are likely to be setbacks. As with any eating disorder the sufferer is likely to need the support of the whole family to pull through to a complete recovery.

In Chapter 7, I explained what the range of services the Eating Disorders Association has to offer. In addition the EDA runs a Telephone Counselling Programme specifically for people with bulimia. It is a structured ten-week programme and sufferers must have the agreement of a GP. Further details are available from the EDA.

Binge eating

Like bulimia, this eating disorder has only recently been recognised by the medical community. It is also called compulsive overeating. Like bulimics, someone suffering from binge eating will binge uncontrollably. However, they will not purge themselves afterwards despite the fact that they experience the same feelings of disgust and self-loathing at what they have just done. Some sufferers graze on high calorie foods throughout the day, but don't eat very much at normal mealtimes. As with most other eating disorders, binge eaters tend to have low self-esteem and are unhappy with some aspect of their lives.

A person may start binge eating at a very young age. It is equally common in men and women, although it is harder to recognise in men and boys because they tend to eat more than their female counterparts anyway. Binge eaters will soon become overweight and some will become seriously obese.

These are some of the things to look out for if you suspect your son might be suffering from binge eating disorder:

- weight gain, which cannot be explained away as puppy fat
- eating very quickly
- always eating large amounts of food
- constantly grazing on high calorie snacks
- eating in secret in the bedroom or elsewhere
- hiding food in the bedroom
- eating like a robot rather than in response to hunger and not really seeming to enjoy the food
- lethargy
- withdrawing socially; overweight children are often teased at school and may choose to spend more time at home doing things on their own
- unexplained mood swings and depression.

Being overweight has many implications for long-term health. The most obvious are heart disease and diabetes. If you suspect your son has a binge eating disorder you should contact your GP, who may refer your son to a specialist for treatment or may suggest that the first step is to try and introduce a healthy eating regime at home with the help of the practice dietician. It is important that both his eating habits and emotional issues are addressed if treatment is to be successful. If it is not offered, you might consider asking your GP to refer your son for therapy to try and address any emotional problems he may have. It is easier for a GP to recognise a binge eating disorder than anorexia or bulimia, because the sufferer is likely to be significantly overweight for his height and age.

Compulsive exercising

It is more common for men to suffer from compulsive exercising disorder than women. Cultural pressures are enormous for boys and young men to be slim and fit and have a muscular physique. Boys in their teens are most at risk of becoming compulsive exercisers. However much they exercise they are still dissatisfied when they look in the mirror. Whereas anorexics strive to be as thin as possible, compulsive exercisers strive for bigger and more defined muscles. It becomes such an obsession that all they want to do is exercise. In the short-term this gives them a feeling of euphoria as the endorphins are released into the body. Longer term they become so obsessed that they continue to exercise even when injured. Many also eat very specialised diets, concentrating on protein to build up muscles and other high-energy diet supplements. Eventually exercise takes over their lives. If they don't exercise they feel depressed and feel they have failed. They use exercise to hide away from, or block out, any emotional problems in their lives.

Things to look out for if you suspect your son is suffering from compulsive exercising are:

- exercising at every opportunity
- long and complicated exercise routines carried out at home
- exercising immediately after eating
- avoiding fatty and other high calorie foods
- asking you to buy him dietary supplements such as high protein shakes
- withdrawing socially in order to spend more time exercising
- exercising even when injured
- lethargy caused by too much exercising
- mood swings and/or depression at times
- low self-esteem
- becoming increasingly body image conscious
- constantly stepping on the scales.

The combination of excessive exercising and a restrictive diet can have some serious health implications. Sufferers can drive themselves to exhaustion; they can suffer from high blood pressure, low body temperature and lower than normal testosterone levels. Young boys and teenagers could stunt their growth and seriously damage their developing joints and limbs. Schoolwork is likely to suffer as they become more and more preoccupied with exercise. Psychologically they are likely to become withdrawn and depressed.

This is a very difficult disorder for parents and GP's to diagnose. Lots of boys take their sport very seriously and love to exercise. However, if you suspect your son is becoming so obsessed with exercise that it is affecting other areas of his life then I recommend that you seek professional help from your GP. Many sufferers want to stop exercise from dominating their lives, but don't know how to.

ED-NOS

This stands for 'Eating Disorders Not Otherwise Specified' and this category includes anyone who has problems with eating but who does not fit neatly within any of the above categories. Examples could include a person who:

- is displaying anorexic tendencies but who is still within the normal weight range

- is binge eating and vomiting, but only on an occasional basis such as once or twice a week

- has a real fear of certain important food types but manages to maintain a reasonable weight by eating other foods

- chews food but then spits it out rather than swallowing it

- has developed rituals around eating but still manages to eat enough to maintain a reasonable weight.

For all these people it is likely that thoughts of food dominate their lives, they are not eating a balanced healthy diet and it is possible that they have emotional issues. It is important not to dismiss problems with food as 'something they will grow out of'. People with ED-NOS are quite likely to develop a more serious eating disorder. If problems are addressed at an early stage then it is much more likely that you can prevent your son from developing a full-blown eating disorder. Try discussing your son's eating habits with him. He may be unaware that his diet is faddy or unbalanced. If he doesn't respond then it is well worth seeking outside help. The EDA can help in several ways as I explained in Chapter 7. If you fail to resolve his issues around food at home, then it is important to ask your GP for a referral to a specialist in eating disorders or to a specialist dietician.

Suggested Reading List

There is so much written about eating disorders in general that when you first look you don't know where to start. My child psychiatrist made a couple of recommendations and I found the EDA list very useful (see below).

These are the specific books that I found very useful.

General background reading and self-help guides

Understanding Eating Disorders (Dr Bob Palmer, The British Medical Association) – you can buy this in most chemists, it is one of the 'Family Doctor Series' and provides an excellent introduction to the world of eating disorders.

Anorexia and Bulimia (Dr Dee Dawson, Vermilion) – this is a parent's guide to recognising eating disorders and taking control. Dr Dee Dawson is Director of Rhodes Farm, the London clinic that has helped hundreds of children with eating disorders. This book provides lots of useful information about eating disorders and treatment options. It also describes what to expect from a specialist in-patient unit. This book prepared me for all the horrors of anorexia and gave me hope that we as a family would pull through it.

Anorexia and Bulimia in the Family (Grainne Smith, Wiley) – this is a self-help guide written by a carer for other carers. It describes how the author coped when her grown-up daughter moved back home and brought with her, anorexia. It is a hard-hitting book, describing in detail just how hard things can get. It also provides many many tips on how to deal with anorexic behaviour and how to survive as a family.

Diet of Despair (Anna Paterson, Lucky Duck Publishing) – this is a very well thought out self-help guide for young people suffering from eating disorders and their families. It gives information and valuable insights on all types of eating disorders. Most importantly it gives a structured plan for recovery.

Carers Guide (Eating Disorder Association) – EDA has produced a Carers Guide, which offers support and reassurance and discusses the difficult emotional issues you may be facing. It passes on the experiences of other carers and also includes the perspective of people who have suffered from an eating disorder themselves. The information is presented in an accessible way, written in short paragraphs with practical ideas.

Overcoming Anorexia Nervosa (Christopher Freeman, Robinson) – this is a self-help guide using cognitive behavioural techniques, written by one of the UK's leading authorities on anorexia nervosa. Many experts believe CB therapy is one of the most effective ways of dealing with the emotional problems associated with anorexia. This book explains CBT and contains a complete self-help programme.

Personal accounts

There are many books written about girls who have suffered from anorexia. I found these two gave me the most insight into the complexities of the illness and what my son was feeling as he became ill and then embarked on the long road to recovery:

Anorexic (Anna Paterson, Westworld International Ltd.) – Anna suffered from anorexia for 14 years. She is very clear that it was triggered by her abusive grandmother. It is a harrowing story of a young girl's fight for survival and the effect on her family. This book gives hope to families who have been coping with anorexia over a long period of time.

The Best Little Girl in the World (Steven Levenkron, Puffin) – this is a fictional book written by one of the foremost experts on anorexia in the USA. It describes how an outwardly happy and well-balanced child can actually be feeling very lonely and left out by the demands of other children within the family.

About men

There are very few books about eating disorders in men, although this is changing and I was delighted when Fit to Die was published in 2004. These are the books I would recommend:

Fit to Die (Anna Paterson, Lucky Duck) – in this book the author draws the reader's attention to the characteristics of and special difficulties for men with eating disorders. If this book had been around when my son was ill I would have felt a lot less lonely and less guilty about my son having developed an eating disorder. I would also have been more prepared as a carer for a male sufferer to cope with the ups and downs of my son's illness.

Making Weight (Anderson, Cohn & Holbrook, Gurze Books) – this book is written by three of the leading experts on eating disorders in males in the US. It describes the explosion in the numbers of men with eating disorders, body image conflicts, compulsive exercise and obesity. This book examines why men have become affected by such issues and what to do about it.

Eating Disorders in the UK: Review of the Provision of Health Care Services for Men with Eating Disorders (Jeanette Copperman, EDA) – this review was commissioned by the Eating Disorder Association and published in 2000. It makes very interesting reading. It found that whilst there was a considerable overlap in what constitutes good practice in the treatment of men and women, there are some important differences in the routes into the illness, vulnerability factors, accessing services and the appropriateness of treatment. It is available free from the EDA by email; printed copies are available for a small fee.

The Eating Disorder Association has a more comprehensive reading list, and a list specifically for males suffering from an eating disorder and their families. You can visit their website at www.edauk.com.

List of Useful Organisations

Eating Disorders Association

First Floor, Wensum House
103 Prince of Wales Road
Norwich NR1 1DW
Telephone Helpline: 0845 634 1414
Youthline: 0845 634 7650
Email: info@edauk.com
Website : www.edauk.com

Anorexia and Bulimia Care

PO Box 173
Letchworth
Hertfordshire SG6 1XQ
Tel: 01462 423 351
Email: anorexiabulimiacare@ntlworld.com
Website: www.anorexiabulimiacare.co.uk

ChildLine

Telephone Helpline: 0800 1111
Website: www.childline. org.uk

YoungMinds

Parents' Information Service 0800 018 2138
Website: www.youngminds.org.uk.

The Samaritans

Telephone Helpline: 08457 909090
Email: jo@samaritans.org
Website: www.samaritans.org.uk

Local services

You might also consider contacting your local volunteer bureau, your health centre, your local hospital, your library, your local newspaper or the Citizens Advice Bureau for information on eating disorder support groups and services in your local area.

Part Two

Joe's Story

14. Setting the scene – happy chaos

An early starter

1989 – My pregnancy with Joe was totally unplanned and caught me by complete surprise. My career was progressing well, and I was enjoying a rapid ascent up the promotion ladder. I had a hectic social life and enjoyed playing hockey every weekend. The pregnancy passed without complication until the 34th week. Then Joe decided enough was enough and decided to make a dramatic entrance into the world. We had just celebrated Christmas with my family, we had nothing prepared and Joe arrived in a rush in a hospital miles from our home. He spent two weeks in the special care unit where he got over some minor early complications very quickly. In mid January we took our beautiful, healthy 6 lb baby boy home.

In the special care unit Joe had seemed quite big compared to some of the other prem. babies, but when we got him home he suddenly seemed so tiny and helpless. I was very nervous to begin with, but the nurses at the hospital had trained me very well in the art of looking after a prem. baby. In no time at all Joe was as strong, healthy and active as any baby that had been born full term. Little did I know that the effects of being born prematurely could manifest themselves much later in life. There is evidence that prem. babies are significantly more likely than full term babies, to suffer from behavioural problems, including eating disorders, in their later years.

Growing up

At six weeks old, on his due date, Joe weighed 3.4 kg (7 lbs 9 oz), which would have been an average birth weight. In fact he still looked very newborn, and was still very crinkly and floaty, but the health visitor was very happy with his progress, and predicted that he would soon start piling on the weight. Sure enough at six months he weighed just under 8 kg, bang on the 50th centile for a six-month-old boy. He remained on the 50th centile thereafter and we stopped having him weighed regularly when he was two years old. I thought that as far as Joe was concerned that would be the end of plotting his weight on average weight charts to check he was in a normal range. I couldn't have been more wrong.

The first major event in Joe's life was when his father went to work abroad. Joe was nearly two years old and I had just discovered I was pregnant. It is fair to say that our marriage was fairly tumultuous, and there were lots of heated debates about whether Joe and I should accompany Steve to Pakistan. I was resisting for a variety of reasons, but mainly because I simply didn't fancy bringing up a young family in Pakistan, nor the isolation I would inevitably suffer as an expat wife in a very alien culture. When I discovered I was pregnant this confirmed my decision to stay in the UK at least until the baby was born. Obviously it wasn't ideal for Joe that his father was so far away, but he seemed happy enough and when Tom was born, Joe was a very proud older brother, with only the occasional hint of jealousy. Steve came back to the UK for a visit shortly after Tom was born and I very quickly realised that I didn't want to join him living abroad. We formally separated three months later, although from Joe's perspective this was no different from his father living abroad and he had already gone through the trauma of getting used to seeing his father on an ad hoc basis. So the boys spent their early years in a lone parent family situation. I had no option but to carry on working but, on the whole, I was lucky to find excellent childminders and nannies, and the boys rarely complained. Financially we were comfortable. I was earning a reasonable salary and we lived in a nice two bedroom house in a cul-de-sac in North London. Apart from the separation from their father, the boys had a comfortable and fairly uneventful upbringing, with a happy and relaxed home environment. Joe grew up into a very active and sporty boy with a healthy appetite. His great passion was football and I spent hours and hours playing with him in the garden, and taking him to the local football sessions on a Saturday morning.

Having to work full time, and bringing up two boys on my own was certainly hard work, but I have always been very organised and managed to juggle the two roles successfully.

Happy chaos

When Joe was eight and a half years old I met a wonderful man, James, who I married two years later. He was, and still is, brilliant with the boys and they certainly responded well to having a man around the house. So we have ended up with quite a large and complex extended family. My second husband has three children from a previous marriage who come to visit every other weekend and for holidays. Joe and Tom have kept in regular contact with their father who spent a short period in the UK after we separated, but then moved back abroad. They have seen him three or four times a year, often travelling to very exotic locations, and normally accompanied by their grandparents. Their father also remarried and has two more children. Whilst this all sounds quite complicated, we all get on and we have had several family occasions where all parties have attended and got on very well.

New school

The next major change for Joe came when he was nine years old. The boys had been attending a small local village school and were very happy there. However, when the head teacher retired it was decided that the school would be closed down and all the children were moved to a much larger school in the local town called St. John's. It was a very good school with much better facilities, but it was a big change for both boys. It was also slightly unusual in that it catered for both the primary and secondary school age groups. It had high academic standards and streamed the boys from an early age. The top streams moved on at a very fast pace. Both boys settled in very quickly and made lots of new friends. Within a year Joe had represented the school at a variety of sports including football and swimming. He had also been put into the top stream, with a group of very bright boys all a year ahead of where they should be. Joe struggled with some of the subjects but managed to hold his head above water and bonded extremely well with the other boys in the class. Joe seemed happy at first, but it became evident later on that he felt very pressurised in this class, and it certainly didn't help when he became ill.

Stretch and grow

2001 – The boys had quite an exciting and busy summer holiday. We took Joe, Tom and their three stepsiblings on a sailing holiday in Turkey, and Joe and Tom went skiing with their father, stepmother and half siblings in New Zealand. On top of this the boys did the normal round of sleepovers, trips to the coast, theme parks etc. The boys reluctantly returned to school in September, but Joe immediately perked up on discovering that he was to be included in the U13 first team for football. This meant he would have two years in this team, something for which he had been aiming for some time, but he was not a hundred per cent sure that he would be included. As a younger member of the team, he was physically smaller, and slower than many of his team-mates, but he more than made up for this with his skills and his intelligent approach to the game. The sports master was very demanding and barked instructions constantly from the sidelines, but the boys were used to this and respected his views. Joe played in the midfield and was renowned for his hard tackling but also made and scored several goals in the season. As well as football Joe religiously turned up for athletics and swimming clubs after school, and the sports masters involved had reported back to me that Joe was showing considerable talent in both areas. With all this activity I wasn't at all surprised to notice that over the course of the autumn term Joe seemed to stretch and grow into a taller and slimmer boy than he had been previously. Joe had never been overweight, but had previously had quite chunky sportsman's legs and thighs. I wasn't concerned at the time as Joe looked the picture of health and continued to devour his meals at home, as well as enjoying a reasonable amount of snacks and drinks in between meals. We were soon to find out that Joe wasn't as happy as he appeared from the outside.

With the benefit of hindsight however, there were several things that happened in that period that may have unsettled any eleven-year-old boy.

- First, in July we moved to a larger house much nearer to the boys' school, but this meant leaving behind the very cosy cul-de-sac in which we had lived for five years and which contained several boys of both Joe's and Tom's ages who had become very firm friends. By coincidence we moved whilst the boys were in New Zealand with their father, so they left one home to return three weeks later to a new home. Our new neighbours had children of Tom's age, but not Joe's, so Joe had to get used to organising to see friends in advance rather than just popping next door.

- Second, in September I stopped commuting up to the City every day and instead worked part-time from home. I felt the boys had outgrown the nanny and it would be in all our interests if I could spend more time with them. So we let the nanny go and I set up an office at home. Tom was ecstatic that I would be at home more and Joe seemed happy, but looking back, he must initially have found it strange having me around all the time, after eleven years of only seeing me in the evenings and at weekends. In addition, working at home meant that my work phone was constantly ringing, which I later discovered Joe felt was a major intrusion into his home life. To begin with I drove the boys to school each morning, but because this was in the prime time for making early morning calls to my clients, I had to resort to having them picked up by taxi. Again, I didn't find out until later how much Joe hated this. Luckily after only a few weeks Sophie, one of the other mums, offered to pick them up each morning.

- Third, whilst Joe was enjoying the sporting side of school life, apart from his main strength – maths – he was not enjoying the academic side. His half term report contained a mixture of A and B grades both for achievement and effort, which was no mean achievement, but the comments from his form teacher noted that he was struggling in this highly academic and competitive group. After half term came the school exams in which Joe came top in his class in maths, but he was in the bottom quartile for French, science, geography, history and RS. Joe was clearly disappointed; despite the fact that I spent some time explaining to him that to be in the bottom quartile in the top stream was nothing to be ashamed of and that in terms of the whole year group his performance still placed him in the top 20%. In addition Joe's end of term report contained several very positive comments, noting that he had worked hard and enthusiastically that term, and performed especially well in maths and of course football. It was only much later I would discover how depressing Joe found it to get yet another exam paper back in which he was placed at, or near, the bottom of the class.

- Finally, my father died suddenly in November. He was 80 years old and had been poorly, but we all thought he would live for another ten years, so it was a shock for everyone. The boys appeared to take it in their stride, but he was, after all, their grandfather and it may have affected Joe more than we realised at the time. In addition, my mother, who has suffered from chronic depression for many years, needed a lot of support through this time and I spent a lot of time tending to her needs, leaving James to cope with the boys.

On top of all these factors Joe was entering a very early puberty. Whilst he was physically still quite small, his voice was starting to break and his body was becoming very hairy. None of his classmates were developing at quite the same rate and it is possible that Joe was feeling very self-conscious about his changing appearance.

Dysfunctional family situation?

Not surprisingly, at a later stage, many observers also suggested that Joe's illness was caused by the fact that we were such a complicated family. Of course family issues are extremely important when trying to establish triggers for an illness like anorexia, and what did become clear later on was that Joe felt immense pressure being the eldest child in a complex family situation. Not only did he have to deal with his very excitable and sometimes challenging younger brother Tom, but also with his three younger stepsiblings every other weekend and his two younger half siblings whenever he visited his father. Joe must sometimes have felt that all these younger children were grabbing all the attention, leaving him to fend for himself as he entered that very confusing prepubescent stage. It is important to note however that anorexia is not just a feature of complex family situations. Anorexia can also affect children from all types of family situation.

A lean Christmas

The autumn term rushed by. The boys went to New Zealand with their paternal grandparents, to see their father. This was the norm for the boys, because if they didn't travel to see their father at Christmas they wouldn't see him from August until Easter the following year. As usual we had our family Christmas celebrations two weeks early and Joe and Tom both tucked in to enormous portions of Christmas lunch. They went off to New Zealand both looking healthy, happy and relaxed, although as I mentioned before Joe had stretched and grown into a taller and slimmer boy than he had been in the past few years.

I spoke to the boys several times over the holiday period and on Joe's twelfth birthday, which fell on December 30th. Those long distance phone calls were always difficult and often the boys could be quite uncommunicative, understandably wanting to keep life with Daddy separate from life with Mummy. On this trip however Joe was even quieter than normal and I did worry that he wasn't particularly enjoying the trip. I realised that he sometimes found it difficult being the eldest child of such a complex family, and found some of the activities with his younger siblings quite tedious and boring, both at home in England, and when visiting his father.

About two weeks into the trip Joe's father called me and said that they were worried about Joe's eating habits. He seemed to be pushing his food around the plate and was more interested in going for a run than eating a proper meal. It was difficult for me to respond to this because I couldn't actually see how Joe was behaving, so I gave what I thought was the best advice I could in the circumstances. "Obviously keep an eye on things, but don't make too much of a fuss about it, as it could blow up into an even bigger issue." I suppose I thought at the time that Joe was being a typically difficult prepubescent boy, who perhaps didn't particularly like the food being served to him. He had said in the past that when he visited his father the food portions were always enormous, with cooked breakfasts and rich puddings being the norm rather than the exception. Little did I realise that Joe was virtually starving himself, whilst also running himself into the ground, and that his father and stepmother were worried that this was the early stages of anorexia.

Rex

The next year of our lives was going to be dominated by a little devil that had wheedled its way inside Joe's head and firmly implanted its vicious horns into Joe's brain. I named this horrible creature Rex.

15. Decline and fall

January 2002 – the early signs

I always felt very excited going to pick the boys up from the airport after a trip to see their father, but when Joe walked through into the arrivals lounge at Heathrow with his brother and grandparents, I tried not to show how shocked I was. He was literally a shadow of his former self. Rather than looking tanned and healthy from three weeks in the sun, he looked gaunt and tired. In contrast Tom looked radiant and was a bundle of energy and happiness, despite having just travelled halfway round the world. On the way home, Tom chattered away happily about all the places they had visited and the things they had done, whilst Joe sat quietly gazing out of the car window.

That afternoon Joe was due to go on a friend's birthday trip to the cinema to see Lord of the Rings. He refused any food before he went, saying he would have loads to eat at the cinema and then he was gone, leaving the rest of us to be entertained by Tom's gleeful antics. Joe continued to be quiet and withdrawn over the next few days, but this was not particularly unusual for him when he was recovering from jetlag. The Christmas trips always seemed to be the most difficult for him to cope with because there was such a short period of time between arriving home and returning to the hectic schedule of school. However, I did notice that on this occasion Joe was avoiding any extra snacks between meals, and on a subsequent trip to the cinema he managed to eat just two fruit pastilles before handing the packet over to me, saying he was 'completely stuffed'. At this stage he was still eating full portions at mealtimes, which I took some comfort in, and I decided not to make too big a deal about the fact he had lost so much weight in those recent weeks.

However, when it came to trying on the school uniform and games kit before the start of term, whilst Tom's all still fitted perfectly, Joe's school clothes were hanging off him. At the end of the previous term I had been predicting that we would need to move up to bigger sizes for Joe following his recent growth spurt, but, apart from having to let his trousers down slightly, his school clothes, if anything, looked too big. I gently persuaded Joe to step on the scales. He weighed 38 kg (just under 6 stone), considerably less than the 42 kg (6 stone 8 lbs) he had weighed in at in one of his science lessons the previous term. He dismissed my fears that perhaps he had lost a little too much weight, saying that he was now exactly the same size as the other boys in his class and that he would be fitter on the sports field. He certainly looked in good shape in terms of his muscle tone. Where he had slimmed down, his muscles were now very clearly defined in his arms and chest, and his legs which previously had been quite chunky, were now much slimmer, but with clear muscle definition. Whilst he looked a little gaunt around the face Joe was clearly happy with his current physique and weight and he assured me that he would eat all his meals to stay healthy, he just didn't fancy eating loads of sweets at the moment. That evening he happily ate a full adult size portion of casserole and although I felt he had lost a bit too much weight over the Christmas break, I hoped that once he was back in a routine at school and eating three large meals a day, then he should put a little of the weight back on. The next day, out of curiosity, I dug out Joe's Child Health Record. According to the weight chart in the book, the average weight for a 12 year old (i.e.: the 50th centile) should be 41 kg; 38 kg was between the 25th and 50th centile, so really Joe had not moved outside the normal range for a boy of his age. As long as he didn't lose any more weight, things should be OK.

Over the next two weeks Joe's weight stabilised, he ate his normal large bowl of cereal for breakfast and a large meal in the evening. He seemed happy at school and at home it was very clear that Joe was proud of his new physique. He started doing pull-ups on the stairs and within days could do twenty with great ease. When his friends came round to play, they would try to compete, but the most anyone else could do was five. It was quite entertaining to watch at first and certainly Joe was getting lots of positive attention from his peers. I started to relax a little and tried to accept that Joe's new physique was a good thing, and something that he was very comfortable with.

Then things started to change. The weather got colder and the school was afflicted by a virulent strain of gastric flu. Whilst Joe continued to eat well at home, he seemed to be losing more weight. He put it down to the fact that he was getting tummy cramps during the day and was finding it hard to eat the school food. According to Joe, virtually his whole class was feeling the same, and I was certainly aware that many of the boys had been staying at home. Over the course of the next two weeks, Joe seemed to lose all his spark and energy, and became quite withdrawn. In the end I decided to take him to the doctor.

Don't mummies fuss?

Given we had only moved to the area six months previously and the fact that Joe is normally a fit and healthy child, this was the first time that our local GP had met Joe. I explained that there was a virus going around at school, but also that I was concerned that Joe had lost so much weight over the past six weeks. The doctor gave Joe a thorough examination and weighed him... 37 kg (5 stone 11 lbs), another kg lost... but apart from commenting on Joe's well-developed six pack, he gave Joe a clean bill of health. He even had a joke with Joe about how Mums fuss, putting me firmly in my place, but he clearly meant well. He was not concerned, and advised Joe to drink plenty of fluids and he should get over the tummy cramps in a few days.

Joe returned to school a few days later, but still seemed poorly. I decided to call his form tutor, a wonderful and very experienced teacher in his mid fifties, who was very popular with the boys. Peter Dunston said he was very glad I had called, because Joe's health had been the topic of much debate in the staffroom in the past week. All of Joe's teachers had noticed a change in his mood and were concerned about his weight loss. I outlined our visit to the doctor and we both agreed that if Joe did not improve over the course of the week I should take him back. If I needed any confirmation from the school over the change in Joe, then Peter was very happy for the doctor to call him direct. Peter gave me his mobile number so that I could contact him anytime. It was a number I would be using regularly over the next few months.

Over the course of the next week Joe deteriorated further and was now clearly struggling to eat his meals at home. I noticed several changes in Joe's behaviour. He was becoming very fussy about any mess around the house and was constantly putting any clutter into neat piles. His bedroom was immaculate. His attitude to hygiene also changed dramatically. I was used to having to cajole him into having a shower every few days, but suddenly he started to shower every night and he would leave the bathroom spotless. Was this a positive side of his early puberty or something more sinister? The doubts started creeping back into my mind.

At the Wednesday afternoon football match I asked one of the other Mums how she thought Joe looked and she confirmed that if Joe were her son she would be worried. I explained that the doctor had given him a clean bill of health, but that I was still concerned. Not only had he lost weight and developed new habits, but also his character seemed to be changing: he had become quite argumentative and at times depressed. My friend agreed with me that I should go back to the doctor. After the match, I spoke to Joe's sports master, Mr Robinson, to ask what his views were. He also agreed that Joe wasn't himself and should try and put some weight back on, and later as Joe and I were leaving the ground, he shouted over to Joe, "Put some weight on boy." Like our doctor, he meant well, but Joe glared at him. I guess he was embarrassed at this public outburst. On the way home I tried to broach the subject, explaining to Joe that it wasn't just a case of me being a fussy Mum, other people were worried about him as well. Joe's response was one of total dismissal, " You can't expect me to listen to what Mr Robinson says, look how fat and out of condition he is." There was not much I could say to this, as Mr Robinson was certainly a larger than life character, who clearly enjoyed his food and drink.

Early the next morning I called the doctor's surgery to make another appointment. This was the last week before half term and we were going skiing on the Saturday, so I wanted to see the doctor before we went. I was given an appointment for 5 pm on Friday 8 February and I hoped the doctor would take my concerns more seriously this time, although I could understand that Joe probably didn't look that ill to someone who had only met him for the first time a week before. When I picked Joe up from school I told him about the appointment, and he simply shrugged and said, "Well Mummy, I don't know why you are making such a fuss, I'm absolutely fine."

Another kg lost

The doctor was more sympathetic on this second visit. Joe's weight had dropped by a further kg to 36 kg (5 stone 9 lbs) and I think the doctor could see that I was genuinely concerned, both about Joe's weight loss and that Joe seemed to be almost depressed at times. The doctor explained to Joe that it wasn't a good idea for a growing boy to lose too much weight and that perhaps he could try and eat a bit more at mealtimes, just to make sure he didn't lose any more weight. Joe agreed that this was a reasonable request and he would try. The doctor also suggested I should get some energy drinks for Joe, which should help boost his energy levels, and of course add a little more to his calorie intake. I think that both the doctor and I believed that Joe would be more relaxed on the skiing holiday, that he would be hungry from all the outdoor activity, and therefore would not be able to resist the highly calorific and fattening ski chalet food. Certainly I hoped that we would return from skiing and I would be able to report back to the doctor that Joe's weight had stabilised, and he was looking much healthier.

Sliding down a slippery slope

We were going skiing with another family from the boy's school. Jacob Holmes was in Joe's class, although he was a year younger than Joe, and an extremely bright boy. Six months previously Joe and Jacob had been almost identical builds, but since then Jacob had filled out, whilst Joe had drastically slimmed down. Jacob's older brother Matthew was very sporty and particularly good at cross-country. Not surprisingly Joe held him up as a role model where running was concerned. Unlike Joe, Matthew had always had a beanpole like figure, despite the fact that he consumed huge amounts of food at every opportunity.

The Holmes had chosen to drive to the ski resort, whilst we were flying. We had to be at the airport early, so once we had checked in we headed for Garfunkels for breakfast. James and I tucked into a full English breakfast, Tom had bacon, beans and toast, but Joe announced he didn't need anything because he had already had some yoghurt at home. I tried to persuade him at least to have some toast because it was going to be a long day, but he refused. I reminded him what the doctor had said about the dangers of losing too much weight, but he got very angry. I ordered him a chocolate milk shake in the hope that he wouldn't classify this as food but he had two sips before claiming he was absolutely stuffed full and couldn't possibly drink any more. I didn't want our holiday to start with a huge fight over food so I backed off. After breakfast I headed for Boots and bought a large tin of high calorie orange glucose drink, which claimed to be packed full of vitamins and minerals and some glucose tablets. I hoped that I could boost both Joe's calorie intake and energy levels over the coming week.

We arrived at the chalet at 7 pm to find the Holmes already settled in. They had stopped off at a supermarket and stocked up on plenty of booze for the adults, and snacks for the children, which evidently Jacob and Matthew had already tucked into with great gusto. Tom's eyes lit up when he saw the stock of goodies, but Joe quietly said, "You'll get really fat if you eat all those," and proceeded to his room to unpack his bag. This comment came from a boy who had eaten a yoghurt for breakfast, a ham roll for lunch and nothing else all day. Hardly enough calories for a toddler let alone a growing 12-year-old boy.

The chalet was run by a charming chalet boy called Simon, who turned out to be an excellent cook. I was pleased to see that even Joe seemed to appreciate the food and at dinner consumed his entire main course in record time, although he declined the gooey chocolate pudding. I also mixed up Joe a glass of the orange drink which he drank, albeit reluctantly. In terms of Joe's food consumption for the rest of the week, this first day pretty much set the standard. He would rise early and have a yoghurt for breakfast, and reluctantly drink his orange. At lunchtime, whilst the rest of us would tuck into a hot meal of pizza or pasta and chips accompanied by mulled wine or hot chocolate, Joe would have a ham or a cheese roll and a small cold drink. On arriving back at the chalet, with the exception of Joe, we would all tuck into French bread and jam, and tea and cakes, whilst Joe would curl up on the sofa to play on his game boy, and again reluctantly have an orange drink. At dinner Joe would eat his main course, but decline pudding, and religiously avoid the snacks, which were rapidly being consumed by the other three boys. My hopes of Joe putting some weight back on rapidly diminished as the week went on. When I suggested to Joe that he should try and eat a little more he snapped back at me, his argument being that Matthew was thinner than he was, so why couldn't I just leave him alone. This was an undisputed fact, but the difference was that Matthew ate constantly and was naturally very thin. In contrast Joe was artificially reducing his weight by restricting his food intake. I broached the subject with Robert who had a medical background, but he advised me not to make a big issue of it, as Joe seemed to be coping on the food he was eating, and this was really an issue we needed to address at home rather than in a holiday situation. This seemed sensible advice so once again I backed off, although I was alarmed at how pale and cold Joe was all the time. Later I found out that both Helen and Robert were very concerned about Joe and could see that we needed professional help, but they didn't want to unduly worry us on the holiday.

An angry young man

In addition to my ongoing concern over Joe's food intake, the other alarming change to occur that week was in Joe's temper. Joe and Matthew were snowboarding, whilst the rest of us were skiing. Matthew was very good at waiting for Joe and giving him tips, but what Joe couldn't get the hang of was picking up enough speed to traverse the flatter sections of the ski runs and, as any skier knows, these are unavoidable. The result was that every so often Joe would either fall over just as he was picking up speed for a flat section, or he would simply come to a grinding halt. In either scenario he would then be faced with a long walk to catch up with the rest of us. To start with James and I would try and help him, either by giving him a tow as we skied past or stopping to keep him company on the walk to catch up with everyone else. However, rather than being grateful for any assistance Joe would use it as an opportunity to get really angry and berate whoever had stopped to help him with language that I didn't even know he knew. His outbursts generally went along the lines of:

"Why are you taking me on these flat bits on purpose?"

"Can't you read the map properly to avoid these flat bits?"

"Don't you get the message that you are making this impossible?"

"Why are you trying to ruin my holiday?"

But all in much more colourful language and said in a very threatening manner. We booked him into a private snowboarding lesson for an afternoon, which he seemed to really enjoy, and certainly improved his technique, but as soon as we encountered the next flat run, the temper came straight back. We threatened to take the snowboard back and swap them for skis, but Joe looked so forlorn at this suggestion, and was generally doing so well on the snowboard that this threat was never pursued. On one occasion when Joe got really angry with me for bringing him to a grinding halt on yet another flat run, Robert stepped in and suggested that the rest of us should ski on ahead, and he would bring up the rear with the two boys on their snowboards.

I wouldn't say the holiday was a disaster, we had lots of good skiing and Joe's snowboarding certainly improved in leaps and bounds, but his lack of appetite, his temper and his ever falling body temperature all gave me cause for concern. I knew that on our return to the UK we would have to go back to the doctor and seek a referral to a paediatrician for some specialist advice.

Decline and fall

On Monday 18th February, Sophie turned up as usual at just after 8 am, to take the boys to school. Having been absent for a week, I had a very busy schedule of work that morning, so I literally waved out the window, and got straight back on the phone. However, I did take a short break on the dot of 8.30 am, in order to ring the surgery and book another doctor's appointment, which was scheduled for 5.30 pm the following day. I took a further break at 11 am to ring Joe's form teacher Peter, who was very concerned to see Joe looking so weak and feeble, but pleased that I was going straight back to the doctor. Almost as soon as I put the phone down, Sophie rang. She was extremely concerned, and reported that Joe had seemed close to tears when he had got out of her car at school that morning. Everyone could see that Joe was very poorly, and becoming very depressed, but what could I do to reverse this alarming change in my eldest son?

Another kg lost

The next day I took Joe back to the doctor. Joe now weighed 35 kg (5 stone 7 lbs), another kg lost. Looking at it another way Joe had now lost a stone in the last three and a half months. I knew this because he had been weighed at school for a science lesson the previous term, and was at the time 42 kg (6 stone 8 lbs). The doctor could also see Joe's mood had changed for the worse, and this time there was certainly no joking about well-developed six packs. He quizzed Joe about his continued weight loss, and Joe replied quietly that he constantly had stomach cramps and this was making it difficult to eat very much. The doctor and I both agreed that Joe needed to see a specialist, and this should be arranged as soon as possible. In the meantime the doctor prescribed a high calorie meal supplement drink called Fresubin, to try to boost Joe's calorie intake.

Can anyone help us?

We went straight to the chemist to pick up the prescription and whilst we were there I also purchased a booklet published in association with the British Medical Association entitled *Understanding Eating Disorders*. Of course nothing had been diagnosed at this stage but I was very well aware that, for some reason, my son was finding it increasingly difficult to eat. It very quickly became clear that the Fresubin wasn't going to be the answer to our problems. Joe saw it as an alternative, rather than a supplement, and so would either attempt to eat a meal or drink the Fresubin, but never both. In contrast the booklet on eating disorders was very useful and gave me some insight into what we might be dealing with if Joe was eventually diagnosed as having anorexia. It stated that whilst only one in ten or fewer of people presenting with an eating disorder is male, the balance between boys and girls is less skewed in the youngest sufferers, that is those in their early teens or even younger. It also stated, however, that diagnosis in the male population can be very difficult because eating disorders are often wrongly thought to afflict only women. It was also at this stage that I contacted two self-help organisations: the Eating Disorder Association and Anorexia and Bulimia Care. They both sent me some useful leaflets and gave me some comforting words of advice, but they couldn't put me in contact with any other families in a similar situation. Nor could they recommend any literature specifically addressing the issue of eating disorders in boys. I felt very lonely.

A nasty knock

The next day I had to go up to Scotland on a marketing trip, so I had arranged for Tom to stay with Sophie and Joe was going to stay with one of his friends, Sam, who was in the same football team. They had an away match and Sam's mum Monica, was going to watch the match and then bring both boys back to her house. I rang Monica that evening and she assured me that Joe was OK but that he had suffered a nasty knock early in the game. The sports master had had to carry him off the pitch and had expressed further concern over Joe's continued weight loss. Apparently a much larger boy had run into Joe and Joe had literally been tossed into the air like a rag doll and landed awkwardly. No permanent damage was done but Joe was clearly shaken, and despite being wrapped up in piles of fleeces and blankets, had become very cold whilst watching the rest of the match from the sidelines. Monica also noticed that Joe had not really touched the match tea, and whilst Joe had made a valiant attempt to eat the hot meal she had served up for the boys that evening, he was clearly struggling. Monica had had Joe to stay on many previous occasions so knew what a healthy appetite he used to have. Sam had also noticed that Joe was struggling with his food and, when Joe was out of the room, said to Monica that he was worried because he had observed that Joe had stopped eating any food at lunchtime at school. This was a further piece of new information that added to my concern.

When I returned from Scotland, I once again rang Mr Dunston, relayed the fact that Joe was being referred to a paediatrician and also broached the subject of school dinners. The school dinners at St John's were renowned for being pretty awful, but as far as I was aware Joe had always eaten them because he was hungry. Mr Dunston assured me that if Joe was having a problem eating them, special meals could be arranged. Several of the other boys had special dietary requirements after all. I agreed to discuss this with Joe that evening.

Joe's reaction to having special school meals was one of pure panic. "Mummy, everyone will think I'm really strange, I don't want to be different from all my friends." I explained that he was different because he had lost so much weight, but he was still adamant that he was now exactly the same size as all his mates and I should stop worrying. I suggested that he should take a packed lunch to school, which might be easier to eat, but this was refused on the grounds that this would also make him stand out. In my frustration I told Joe that he would have to come home for lunch then and to my surprise he readily agreed to this. From then on I picked him up every day at 1 pm, and dropped him back to school at 2 pm, and at least I could see that he was eating some lunch every day.

Fading away

The appointment with the paediatrician was scheduled for the 7th March. Whilst it was only just over two weeks away it seemed like an eternity. Over that time, despite coming home for lunch every day, Joe's weight, mood and behaviour changed dramatically. His weight plummeted as he reduced his food intake slightly as each day passed. By the end of February he was consuming less than 1,000 calories a day. Breakfast used to be a huge bowl of cereal, but had now been reduced to part of a Muller Light Yoghurt. Lunch used to be a full meal at school with pudding, but now Joe just managed to eat part of a ham sandwich, part of a banana and part of a chocolate bar. Dinner used to be an adult sized hot meal, but now was a few morsels of pasta, with a couple of mouthfuls of chicken, mince or fish finger. Joe used to drink regularly throughout the day, but now was limiting his intake to half a glass of water or squash with each meal. The more I tried to persuade Joe to eat, the angrier he would get. When I pointed out that if he carried on like this he would end up in hospital, he would fly into a rage and then eat nothing. If I tried gentle persuasion Joe would curl up on the floor clutching his stomach stating that it hurt so much he couldn't possibly eat another thing.

Socially Joe was still seeing his friends, but it was reported back to me on several occasions that he was standing back observing their antics rather than joining in. He would say he was too cold to go outside to play football or too tired to take part in an indoor game of table tennis. He seemed happiest watching TV or playing computer games. Several of his friends commented to their mums that Joe had really changed. Without exception, it was reported back to me by the mums that Joe struggled to eat much at all when he visited their houses, and he would pre-empt any comment by warning his host that he couldn't eat very much.

Joe was still managing to go to school, but only just. I spoke to Mr Dunston on a daily basis. He was very supportive and clearly very concerned over Joe's decline. He tried to encourage Joe to have drinks and snacks at breaktimes, but with varying degrees of success. He also pointed out to me that Joe's writing had become very flowery since returning from skiing. When he asked Joe why he was writing in such an elaborate, and slow and laborious way, Joe simply replied that it made him feel better.

March 11th 02.

History Prep

24. In 1674, two skeletons were found in a chest (both children). The chest was found at the foot of the stairs. very deep, under a great heap of stones. This is the exact place that Sir Thomas M ore said the the brothers were buried.

25. Sir James Tyrell told Sir Thomas More about the murder of the princes.

Tears all round

On several occasions over the next two weeks I was called by matron to come and collect Joe from school because he was feeling poorly or upset. On one such occasion Joe had burst into tears in the Latin lesson. They were putting together menus in Latin and I can only assume that the thought of all the rich food was too much for him to cope with. Seeing Joe once again crumpled up on matron's sofa was too much for me to cope with. I managed to get Joe to the car and drive out of the school grounds, but then I had to pull in to the side as I burst into floods of tears. I felt so helpless. Why was my son, who used to have such a healthy appetite, now starving himself, and literally disappearing in front of my eyes? Joe was devastated to see me so upset. "Mummy, please stop crying, I'll do whatever you want, I'll eat anything you give me, just please stop crying." So, I pulled myself together and drove home. Joe had a small snack when we got home and then asked if we could go for a walk in the local park. This was soothing for both of us, and whilst not much was said between us, I felt closer to Joe than I had for some time. However, just a few hours later, Joe was once again refusing to eat more than a few mouthfuls of his dinner. The demon was back.

The appearance of rituals

I also noticed a further dramatic change in Joe's behaviour over those two weeks as he became obsessive, superstitious and increasingly depressed. Joe had always been very fit and it was not unusual to see him tearing around the garden with his football, doing somersaults on the trampoline, riding his bike up and down the road, or even doing some sit-ups, pull-ups or press-ups around the house. Since our return from skiing, however, Joe had become obsessed with doing the latter three exercises on an almost continual basis. Every time he passed the foot of the stairs on the way to or from the kitchen he would do at least twenty pull-ups. Every time he went up or down stairs he would do twenty to thirty pull-ups halfway up the stairs. After every meal he would do thirty to forty sit-ups and press-ups.

In addition to this very obvious exercise Joe also started doing more subtle activities and sometimes I don't think he even realised he was doing them. If he was sitting on the sofa or in the car, he would sometimes sit bolt upright, constantly tapping his feet or tensing his stomach muscles. He would often count on his fingers, whilst gently rocking backwards and forwards.

Other rituals appeared soon after the exercising had started. Joe would step carefully over the boundaries between each room, as if stepping on the metal strip might cause an explosion. He would go up and down stairs one at a time placing his right foot, quickly followed by his left on each individual step. Joe developed a shuffle in his walk and within a few weeks could not walk without dragging his left foot along the ground behind him. As he shuffled around the house he would touch the walls and surfaces as if this was in some way protecting him against something terrible.

Joe became obsessively clean and tidy. At 7 pm on the dot he would disappear into the shower, to emerge half an hour later, his skin red raw from scrubbing. The bathroom would be left spotless with the towel hanging perfectly on the rail. During the day he would wash his hands meticulously every time he went to the bathroom.

Joe established a strict routine for dressing and undressing. Everything had to be in a particular order and each step was carefully performed before moving on to the next item of clothing.

Every night before going to sleep Joe would read his Dorling Kindersley children's bible. He had had it for years and it had sat neglected on his bookshelf, but now it had become his constant bedtime companion, and he clearly took great comfort from reading it. He would read out loud, tracing each word with his finger.

Joe even developed rituals outside the house. He would go out of his way to walk around lampposts, post boxes or rubbish bins, and he became obsessive about picking up litter, however disgusting that litter might be. He just couldn't bear to see any mess or disorder around him.

As the days went by, Joe withdrew from his school friends and became increasingly clingy to me. As long as I wasn't trying to get him to eat, he would cuddle up to me and follow me round the house, talking about nothing much, but just wanting my constant attention. At times it was like having an overgrown toddler in the house. At other times it was like having a monster in our midst.

As Joe's food intake decreased, the rituals increased; he became increasingly depressed, was often tearful and his physical appearance deteriorated. His skin was dry and scaly, his hands red raw from constant washing and the fact that he constantly chewed on his knuckles. He often appeared to be in a trance and was constantly tired, and always freezing cold. In the latter stages he couldn't even swallow his own saliva and would save it up in his mouth to spit out at an appropriate moment. On occasion he would dribble down his jumper, but this didn't seem to bother him.

Shock tactics – 'You are going to kill yourself'

I felt so useless as I watched my son deteriorate day by day. I had tried gentle persuasion, but this got me nowhere. I had tried the emotional blackmail route, but whenever I cried Joe would promise to eat, only to find out shortly after that he simply couldn't fulfil his promise. I had tried direct confrontation but this always ended in tears and inevitably Joe would eat less, and exercise more to punish me for being such a cruel and heartless mother.

So, I resorted to shock tactics. I took photos of Joe in his underwear and made him count the bones sticking out of his emaciated frame but this had little effect. Joe simply commented that other boys at school were bony too. I tried to explain that Joe could stunt his growth if he carried on like this but it fell on deaf ears.

I tried to explain that people who starved themselves would eventually die but Joe told me not to be so stupid. We ended up having a huge row, which left us both in a dishevelled heap:

"Joe, if you don't eat you are going to die."

"Mummy, stop being so stupid. I'm fine. I just can't eat much at the moment. Why can't you just leave me alone?"

"Because I love you and I don't want to lose you. You have to start eating or you will collapse. You can't even walk upstairs properly. How can you think you will be fit for the cricket season?"

I started shouting to try and get through.

"You're a mess Joe. Look, you are even dribbling all down your jumper. Can't you see what you are doing? What can I say to make you see sense? You need to start eating and stop doing all those ridiculous exercises. You are going to kill yourself."

Joe screamed back.

"Shut up. Shut up. Leave me alone. I can't eat. I can't do anything. My stomach hurts. My head hurts. Stop shouting at me. Leave me alone."

By this time we were both in floods of tears, and needless to say Joe didn't eat any of his next meal.

So I gave up and resorted to tender loving care, with no confrontation and lots of cuddles. I just hoped that this would be enough to keep Joe going until we got help from the medical profession. We quickly learnt that there was no point having huge rows with Joe. Everyone ended up being upset and it achieved nothing.

Watch out for Rex

By this time, I was pretty sure that Joe was suffering from a severe case of anorexia. I had a vivid and frightening dream, almost like a vision, from which I emerged shaken and upset but determined that we would win this battle against an illness that was having such a devastating impact on our whole family.

I dreamt that there was a cheeky little devil called Rex, whose mission was to lure young boys to their early death by persuading them to stop eating. He was a charming and mischievous fellow, with a real glint in his eye and an irresistible manner. In my dream he had caught Joe on a hook and was literally reeling him in like a fish. He had already succeeded in luring him away from home and school. The medical profession was like a boulder in his way, but he was doing everything in his power to maintain the momentum and eventually lure Joe to a very premature death. In my dream there were ghostly images of Joe as he was lured down the slippery path. At home and school was an image of a healthy and happy boy. In the GP's office and the specialist sessions, Joe's image was becoming fainter and visibly thinner. The image of Joe in hospital was almost translucent and his frail body frighteningly emaciated. The next image was of a crumpled skeleton, with a triumphant Rex gloating over his latest prize.

It is often said that anorexia is not like any normal illness, but more like a person who gets inside your head and takes over your life. Your normal, rational personality is pushed aside and your every thought and action is dictated by this intruder. If the intruder is left to his or her own devices you will go on to starve yourself and eventually die. For girls the obvious name for this intruder is Anna. For Joe, after my dream, I found myself calling the intruder Rex.

Most of the time throughout Joe's illness, I managed to maintain a positive outlook, but it is a fact that some sufferers of anorexia go on to die, and on several occasions during March of 2002 I feared for Joe's life. Some studies have indicated that in the very severe population as many as 10 or even 20% will die, either from the effects of starvation or suicide, although others suggest a death rate nearer to 1%. I tried to ignore these figures, as there are so many different definitions of the population, that to a layperson such as myself, the figures are really meaningless. However, in the darker moments, when Joe was very ill and in a desperate state, I did wonder if we would ever beat this terrible disease.

Despair, anger and hate

As a family we were in pieces. It seemed that all my emotional energy was being consumed by Joe and whatever terrible illness had taken over his body and mind. James was incredibly supportive but felt so helpless. Tom simply withdrew into his bedroom and would only appear if he knew Joe was taking a shower or had gone to bed. He was much more subdued than normal and I knew he was struggling to concentrate at school, but what could I do? I tried to reassure him that his big brother would soon get better, that I loved him just as much as ever, despite the fact that Joe was demanding all my attention. Hopefully, we could become a normal family again soon, but I wasn't at all sure how we would achieve this.

Negative thoughts kept going round and round my head. It was almost as if Rex had got into my mind too:

'What have I done wrong? Why can't I make Joe eat? Why can't I stop his excessive exercise and obsessive habits? I'm losing him. He's slipping away before my very eyes. He looks so sad, so lost, so ill. I can't seem to get through, even when he's cuddled up to me, but then he's like a baby who can't understand the simplest of concepts. I'm so scared of losing him. Rex is stealing him away from us. Please give me my son back. I'm so scared. I'm so scared.'

Joe was similarly in complete turmoil, but his was expressed in anger and hate, rather than despair.

'I hate my mum who never leaves me be. I hate the doctors and my teachers who nag me to eat. Everyone wants me to get fat. What's wrong with them? Can't they see I look normal? I can't do sport at the moment because I've got a horrible tummy bug. It hurts to eat. Anyway I hate food. I hate swallowing. It feels so wrong to swallow anything, even my saliva. The voice in my head is telling me I'm right. Mummy calls him Rex. I don't know why. She really hates him and wants him to go away, but he's my only friend and ally. He makes me feel better when everyone else is so upset with me. He tells me that when I feel better and am doing brilliantly at sport, everyone will shut up. They will see how fit and healthy I am, and they will stop trying to make me fat. I'm so tired of people nagging at me. I'm so tired, I'm so tired.'

16. The diagnosis – watch out for Rex

The paediatrician and the child psychiatrist

In the end I couldn't hold out until the 7th March for the paediatrician's appointment. Joe was deteriorating so quickly that each day seemed increasingly precious. I rang the doctor and literally begged for an earlier appointment and he managed to fit us in to see a different paediatrician on 1st March.

The first diagnosis

The paediatrician was very professional and we quickly ran through Joe's background. Having established the history he undertook a full medical examination of Joe. Joe's weight had indeed plummeted to 32.6 kg (5 stone 2 lbs), now just above the 10th centile on the weight charts, whilst his height of 149 cm was exactly on the 50th centile. In addition his blood pressure of 70/40, and his pulse of 60 were both abnormally low. The paediatrician felt that Joe was indeed exhibiting features of anorexia, but we both agreed that other possibilities should be excluded. This involved taking blood, to which Joe's reaction was extreme. He became very tearful and upset as soon as the mention of a blood test was made and when the needle was inserted he became almost inconsolable. He sobbed and sobbed as the blood was being extracted, saying it felt like his life was being sucked out. He was genuinely petrified and clearly thought that this simple procedure could kill him.

No sport and lots of tender loving care

Once the ordeal was over, Joe got dressed and we both sat down to discuss what the next steps would be. Obviously the blood tests would take a few days to come back, but I was horrified when the paediatrician announced he was going on holiday for two weeks and so would see Joe on his return. I wanted to scream. Two more weeks could be two more kg off Joe's already emaciated frame. The paediatrician advised me that Joe should not do any sport, but if he felt strong enough there was no reason why he shouldn't go to school. I should carry on trying to encourage Joe to eat, but basically the best thing I could do for him at this stage was to give him lots of tender loving care. If I was concerned at any stage I should refer back to the doctor. Joe was very quiet and tearful when we left the hospital, presumably exhausted from his ordeal.

The one positive thing to come out of our experience with the paediatrician is that Joe started talking to me about his physical decline. It was as if our trip to the paediatrician had made him realise how ill he really was. He talked mostly when we were walking in the park and I could see a tiny glimmer of hope that perhaps my very sick child might actually be starting to want to get better, whereas previously he had been in complete denial that anything was wrong. He spoke to me about how he wanted to lose some weight before Christmas so he would be a better sportsman and that a couple of boys had teased him about having a fat bum, which he found upsetting. He told me he had lost lots of weight in New Zealand because he didn't really like the food and so he took the opportunity to eat minimal amounts. When he returned from New Zealand he had felt fitter and healthier, and some of his friends had complimented him on his new slim line physique, and that made him feel good. He also talked about being in the streamed class and that he found it so hard to compete with the really bright boys. His self-esteem had also reached an all time low and he claimed on several occasions that he was very stupid.

Meanwhile, Joe's condition continued to deteriorate and on 7th March I was back on the phone to our doctor who gave us an emergency appointment that day. He had the results of the blood tests, which were all essentially normal, but Joe's heart rate was still slow and by this stage Joe had virtually stopped going to school because he was so weak. Joe was spending much of each day curled up in front of the TV, doing his compulsive exercising, going for short walks with me in the park and eating enough to keep a sparrow alive. I had learned that there was an excellent eating disorder unit for children at Great Ormond Street hospital, and so I asked if it would be possible for Joe to be referred there for an assessment. The doctor agreed to look into this. In addition, after consultation with another paediatrician, he organised for Joe to have an abdominal ultra-sound scan and x-ray to rule out the possibility of any abdominal abnormality or blockage, that could be causing Joe's constant stomach cramps. These investigations passed without a hitch and showed no evidence of any abnormality. Unfortunately, however, some further blood tests were also needed which caused Joe just as much distress as the previous ones. Once again we both returned from the hospital feeling totally exhausted and I took Joe back to the doctor the next day, because I was so worried about both his physical and mental condition. The doctor assured me that Joe was still stable enough to be kept at home, but agreed that we needed urgent specialist assistance from the medical profession to have any chance of getting Joe back on his feet.

Because the paediatrician was still on holiday, the doctor referred Joe directly to our local Child & Family Mental Health Unit, and this is where we first encountered the child psychiatrists. On the 13th March I received a phone call from one of the consultants at the unit. She had already spoken to our GP and so was fully aware of Joe's dramatic physical decline over the past few months. By this stage Joe could hardly walk upstairs and was very clingy to me all the time. I also updated the consultant on Joe's mental state. He was now very depressed and constantly tearful. I explained to her that I was starting to feel desperate. I could see my son starving himself to death and there seemed little I could do to stop it. She was very sympathetic and assured me that she would call me back that day to arrange for Joe to be assessed as soon as possible. Half an hour later she called back and advised me that we had been given an appointment with one of her fellow consultants the next morning. This initial assessment would probably last about one and a half hours.

The next morning we headed off to the hospital where we were due to see Dr Davis, the child psychiatrist, at 10 am. Joe was quiet in the car and was obviously nervous about seeing yet another doctor. I was feeling nervous too but tried not to let this show. We had to park in an NCP car park about ten minutes' walk from the hospital and by the time we arrived at the hospital Joe was looking exhausted, and even paler than normal.

I took to Dr Davis straight away. He was incredibly professional, whilst also being very warm and sympathetic. Because of this combination he was very easy to talk to and he had soon built up a picture of our family background and Joe's life history. He seemed to ask all the right questions, and when I later saw a copy of his report of our meeting I was amazed at how he had quickly built up a very accurate picture of the events leading up to Joe's illness. For the first part of the assessment Dr Davis saw both Joe and me together. Joe didn't volunteer any information, but seemed happy to answer direct questions, but generally I did most of the talking in this session. Then Dr Davis had a session with Joe on his own and it was clear from his report of this session that he had managed to get Joe to talk quite openly about his illness, and what had happened in his life over the last few months. Joe admitted to Dr Davis that he was now too skinny but that he didn't know what weight he should be, and he was scared of putting too much weight back on. When I was called back into the room it was clear that Joe had been crying but he seemed to have pulled himself together.

We then moved to another room where Dr Davis weighed measured and examined Joe. His weight was now 31.4 kg (4 stone 13 lbs), which put him just below the 10th centile on the weight charts. I knew from my background reading on eating disorders that this indicated a dangerously emaciated child In contrast his height of 1.495m was exactly on the 50th centile.

We returned to Dr Davis's office and he concluded our meeting. He told me I was quite right to be extremely worried about Joe's condition, and that he felt Joe had severe anorexia and was in need of an in-patient admission so he could embark on a controlled re-feeding programme. He knew that I had already enquired about the Eating Disorder Unit at Great Ormond Street hospital, but pointed out there was also an excellent Adolescent Unit in our county, which might be more suitable for Joe and would be easier for the family to visit. I agreed that this sounded sensible so he rang them to see if he could get us an appointment. It was arranged for the following Tuesday, 19th March, so we just had the weekend to get through. Dr Davis then advised Joe that he shouldn't be exercising at all and stated that many clinicians would advise total bed-rest at his current low weight. He also advised Joe to try really hard to increase his calorific intake over the next few days, so that he could be a little stronger for his inevitable move into the Adolescent Unit. Joe said he would try but wasn't sure how much more he could eat. Dr Davis advised me to carry on being as supportive as I could in the next few days, but if I was worried about Joe's condition, I should take him straight back to our GP and also keep Dr Davis informed.

Both Joe and I felt exhausted after our session with Dr Davis, but at least he had a clear plan of action to help Joe get better. Joe said to me in the car that he didn't really want to go to an in-patient unit but he would try it for a short while if I thought it would help him to get better. Of course at this stage I didn't realise how long Joe would be an in-patient, and so I made lots of encouraging comments about how I felt a short stay in the unit would really get Joe back on the road to recovery.

That afternoon when we picked up Tom from school, Joe was very quick to ask who had won the house cross-country competition that was being held that afternoon. Joe's arch running rival Andrew Cox had won easily. Joe looked forlorn. "I was going to win that race Mummy," he said. "Maybe next year," I replied hopefully. Tom devoured an enormous dinner and then the three of us strolled up to our local McDonald's to get both boys a McFlurry. Joe seemed relatively relaxed and I was pleased he had managed to eat a little more today. Joe had obviously listened to the words of advice from Dr Davis, the child psychiatrist.

No room at the adolescent unit

On Monday of the next week I was distraught to receive a letter from Dr Davis, which informed me that the meeting on Tuesday might have to be postponed because two other referrals had come in. Dr Davis suggested in the letter that I should phone him the following Thursday or Friday to update him on Joe's progress.

I couldn't possibly wait that long, as Joe was fading away in front of my eyes and we had both been clinging onto the fact that the assessment on Tuesday would result in an in-patient admission, and the start of Joe's recovery. The letter gave no indication as to when we might get another appointment: one week, two weeks, a month perhaps? I rang Dr Davis immediately, but as luck would have it he was going to be tied up in meetings all afternoon. I explained to his secretary that I was extremely worried about Joe and she promised to speak to Dr Davis in between his meetings to find out whether or not the assessment had had to be postponed or not. There followed an hour of silence in which I tried to keep my agitation from Joe, who was being very clingy and just wanted to cuddle up on the sofa. When the phone did eventually ring I leapt out of my skin and rushed into the other room so Joe wouldn't hear the conversation. Thankfully the news was positive; we still had an appointment the next day. I was so relieved and thanked Dr Davis's secretary profusely for going to the trouble to chase this up for me. Joe was none the wiser and when I went back into the family room I found him curled up fast asleep on the sofa. At least in sleep he looked peaceful; taking a break from the obsessive rituals that had recently become such a major part of his life.

My husband James took the next day off work so he could accompany Joe and me to the assessment. Since James had come into our life six years earlier, James and Joe had always had a very close relationship. They loved playing and watching all types of sport together, and James had spent a lot of time helping Joe with his maths and Latin homework, which had yielded very positive results at school. For me it was a huge comfort to have James accompany us on that day.

The assessment was being held at the day centre of the adolescent unit. The residential centre, which was a converted barn, was about half a mile away and accommodated up to ten patients at a time. The receptionist explained that the residents came to the day centre each weekday for education and to see therapists etc. Our meeting was with Dr Cornwall, a child psychiatrist, and Suzie Jones, manager of the adolescent unit. The meeting took the same format as the one with Dr Davis, with the first part of the meeting being a general discussion of the events leading up to Joe's illness and his recent dramatic decline. Then James and I left the room so that Dr Cornwall and Suzie could talk to Joe on his own. During the meeting Joe spoke in a weak, high, light voice and was constantly tearful. Joe was extremely agitated throughout the meeting, although he did say that he felt a little calmer this week since seeing Dr Davis, and he had found it a little easier to eat, albeit only small amounts of bland food such as sandwiches and ice cream. He explained that he wanted to beat the illness, but that he was finding it very difficult to swallow, and was salivating a lot. In addition he was finding it difficult to drink much as it made him feel very full and uncomfortable, and he explained that after eating or drinking he felt absolutely compelled to exercise to get rid of the bloated feeling. While Dr Cornwall listened very carefully to Joe's responses, she also made a note of his outward appearance. His fingernails were very bitten and the skin on his hands was very dry. During the meeting he chewed on his nails and knuckles constantly. She noted that he had fine lanugo hair on his arms and face. During the meeting he also displayed obsessive tendencies: he was counting constantly on his fingers, moving his leg up and down, and had an alternate blinking tic of each eye. Of course these are all classic signs of anorexia and severe malnutrition.

Joe was with Dr Cornwall and Suzie for half an hour, and then James and I were called back into the room. Joe looked absolutely exhausted and more like a very frail nine-year-old, rather than a sporty 12-year-old. Dr Cornwall explained that both she and Suzie were very concerned about Joe's physical condition and that he required in-patient admission urgently. However, due to the limited places at the unit, and the fact that two other referrals were being seen that day, they could not offer us a place immediately. Dr Cornwall could clearly see the panic in my eyes and reassured us that she would do everything in her powers to get Joe admitted as soon as possible, but in the meantime we should take him home and keep him as calm and settled as possible. The advice as always was to return to our GP if we were worried about any further decline.

All three of us were quiet on the journey home. Joe could hardly keep his eyes open and seemed to be in a trance. I was beside myself with worry and anxious as to how Joe's father Steve would react to the news of our meeting. Steve was flying in to the country that day. James didn't really know what to say.

Steve arrived at the house about an hour after we did. He was visibly horrified at Joe's appearance, but tried not to show his feelings in front of Joe. Joe was pleased to see his father, but really didn't have the energy to say anything or show much emotion. He simply sat curled up on the sofa and let his father hug him for a while. James kept himself busy in the kitchen, making some sandwiches for lunch. Joe managed to eat half a ham sandwich before returning to the sofa, and then James and I relayed the events of our meeting to Steve. Steve was understandably angry that we had been sent home with no idea as to when Joe might be admitted. I explained about the shortage of beds, and the fact that the medical professionals had to prioritise on a case by case basis, but I felt my words were falling on deaf ears. Perhaps Steve felt I should have been more forceful, or that things would have been different if he had been in the meeting that morning. He was obviously weary after his long trip, and very worried about Joe. All I could say was that I was doing everything in my powers to get Joe back on the road to recovery and that I hoped that my ex husband would support me, rather than fight me in achieving that aim. Steve had clearly been reading up on anorexia, and had his own ideas about how things should progress. James calmed the atmosphere somewhat by reminding me that it was only an hour until Tom needed picking up from school, so if we wanted to take Joe for his normal gentle walk in the park, we should go now. James stayed at the house, whilst Steve and I took Joe over to the park. Joe shuffled along slowly, and Steve and Joe were soon having a conversation about football... Who was going to win the Cup and the League that year?... Probably not Spurs or Liverpool, the teams that Steve and Joe respectively supported.

Emergency admission

Then we picked up Tom from school. He was hugely excited at seeing his father, and when we got home Tom dragged Steve upstairs to show him all his favourite possessions in his bedroom. Joe looked terrible and almost collapsed onto the sofa. I sat down to give him a reassuring hug, but he burst into tears, and through his sobs he said, "Mummy I feel really awful, and my chest hurts." When I sat back to look at him, I saw that his face had a definite green pallor, a clear sign of serious starvation, and his breathing was getting very shallow in between his sobs. I called to James who agreed that this was serious and he rang the GP's surgery to say we would be bringing Joe in. Steve came with Joe and me to the surgery, and we left a very confused Tom with James. We only had to wait a couple of minutes before we saw the doctor, I think the receptionist must have relayed to him how awful Joe looked. Joe could hardly keep his eyes open and seemed to be drifting off into a trance. I explained that we had seen Dr Cornwall that morning, but that she had sent us home with Joe because there was currently no room at the adolescent unit. I also explained that I felt very uncomfortable about keeping Joe at home when he was clearly so ill, and that I was worried he could have a heart attack in the night. The doctor agreed that Joe was showing signs of bradycardia (heart beating at less than 60 beats a minute) and this fact together with the chest pains, constant shivering and Joe's generally very weak condition, meant that he should be admitted to hospital immediately. Having established that we were happy to take Joe to the local hospital ourselves, he rang the paediatric ward and informed them of our imminent arrival. I rang James who threw some overnight things in a bag for both Joe and me, and we picked these up on our way to the hospital.

When we arrived at the paediatric unit the nurses and registrar were waiting, ready to assess whether Joe needed to go straight into intensive care or whether he could stay on the general ward. To my relief, they chose the latter, as I knew that Joe would have really freaked out if he had been rushed into a specialist unit and connected up to a whole array of strange machines, possibly with tubes and needles, as well as electronic monitors. After the registrar had carried out a basic assessment of Joe's condition, I had to fill in several forms and answer all the usual questions about Joe's medical history and the recent events leading up to his current condition. Meanwhile one of the nurses took Joe and Steve to a small ward with just two beds, kitted out with a TV and a small snooker table. The idea was that Joe would share this ward with a boy of a similar age who had been admitted suffering from an asthma attack. Apparently this child was a regular overnight visitor to the ward, knew all the nurses really well and therefore was totally relaxed in these surroundings. In contrast, this was all very strange for Joe, and by the time I had completed all the forms, and answered all the questions, Joe had become almost hysterical at the thought of having to stay the night in this strange place with this strange boy. Joe had been taken off to another room to be weighed whilst I was filling in the forms, and his weight had slipped even further to 31.1 kg. I hoped that now he was in hospital his weight would not slip any further. Joe looked so frail and frightened when he returned to the ward, and he tried to bury his head in my chest so he wouldn't have to face the other people in the room. He felt like a wasted bag of bones.

The nurses were extremely sympathetic and suggested that Joe should move to a smaller room next door, in which he would be the only patient, and it meant that I could stay with him overnight on the sofa bed. Both Joe and I were relieved that I would be able to stay. About an hour later Steve left and I rang James to update him. I was pleased to hear that Tom had eaten a hearty supper and enjoyed a long game of table tennis with James before going to bed. James had reassured him that now Joe was in hospital he would soon start to feel better, and Tom was now sound asleep.

Joe and I had missed the evening meal in the ward, and so the nurse showed me where I could make some toast. Joe managed half a slice, but was still feeling really poorly and not at all like eating. A little later a doctor came to see Joe, and decided that part of the reason for him feeling so poorly was the fact that he had become very dehydrated and therefore should have a drip, at least overnight, if not during the next day or so as well. This was to cause another major upset. Joe was adamant that he was not dehydrated, how could he be if he had saliva in his mouth? Of course the only reason he had saliva in his mouth was because he was finding it difficult to swallow anything and preferred to spit any saliva out into the sink. This in turn was exacerbating his dehydration. I did my best to calm Joe down and the doctor managed to get the needle into the back of Joe's hand and attach the drip. Within minutes Joe was beside himself with anguish. He was reacting in the same way that he had reacted to having blood taken, although in this instance he could feel the fluid running into his veins and this felt totally alien to him. "Mummy I feel like a robot, I'm not a real person anymore." He sobbed for nearly an hour, until he finally lay back down on his bed and drifted into a very fitful sleep. By this time it was nearly 11 pm and whilst I was emotionally shattered, my mind was buzzing, trying to rationalise everything that was happening and worrying about what the future would hold for this very sick child, who was a shadow of my eldest son that I loved so much. I wondered down the corridor, and found the doctor who had seen Joe earlier. She was writing up her notes, and I asked her if she would like a cup of tea. She accepted gratefully, obviously tired after a long day. She chatted to me for about twenty minutes while we drank our tea, and reassured me that Joe would be fine. Now that he had been admitted to hospital, he was much more likely to get a place at the adolescent unit, and if there was no space there, they would soon find somewhere else suitable for him to go. It was clear that he needed in-patient treatment, so I needn't worry about having to take him home and watch helplessly as he continued to starve himself. These were very comforting words, and when I went back to Joe he was sleeping more peacefully. I made up the sofa bed and settled myself down for the night.

Joe stayed on the paediatric unit for three nights in total and each night the drip was reattached to try and keep him rehydrated. He ate enough to keep his weight stable and the bed-rest seemed to do him some good. Some of his school friends came to visit, and brought him a whole array of sporting magazines to keep him occupied and Steve brought Tom in each day after school to see his brother. It was the last week of term, so Tom had plenty of end of term news to relay to Joe. In addition Tom was going on the school ski trip that weekend and so his excitement about that meant that he didn't have too much time to worry about what Joe would be doing while he was away.

On the second day of Joe's stay at the paediatric unit we were given the wonderful news that Dr Cornwall had managed to get Joe a place at the adolescent unit. He was to be admitted on Friday afternoon, so it was arranged that Joe would be discharged from the paediatric ward on Friday morning. We would take him home first to pick up all the things he would need for his stay at the adolescent unit. I discussed this with Joe at length and he genuinely seemed to want to get better. He understood that he could not do this at home, and he said he would do whatever he was told, in order to get better as quickly as possible. At this stage neither of us realised how long his stay at the adolescent unit might be. Neither did we realise how upsetting the extraction of Joe from the family would be. Over the last few months Joe had become extremely clingy to me, and in the last few weeks we had been inseparable. Both of us would find the forthcoming separation very traumatic.

Love and hope

Now that Joe seemed to want to get better, I felt we must have reached rock bottom. I began to think more positive thoughts:

> 'I love my son so much and I know that we can pull through this together. It's going to be really tough, and I'm sure there will be some horrible setbacks on the way, but we are a strong family unit. There is lots of love and that will be what will bring us all out the other side. There is hope. We can beat Rex.'

Joe started to think more positively as well, despite being so frail:

> 'I love my mum. I know she's trying to help me. It's just so hard. I want to get better. I want to play sport again, but I'm terrified of getting fat. The voice in my head is still there, taunting me whenever I try to eat. But I love my mum and my family and my friends. I want to get better. I can get better. I can beat this.'

17. The treatment – heaven or hell?

On Friday March 22, 2002 Joe, weighing just 31.3 kg, was admitted to The Great Barn Adolescent Unit. The layout of the ground floor of The Great Barn was open plan, with a dining area at one end and a spacious lounge at the other. I noticed that there were several videos on the shelf that we had at home and a football book, which I hoped would help Joe settle in. On our arrival The Great Barn was very quiet as the other patients had either already gone off for weekend leave or were still at the education centre.

Whilst we were waiting to meet the nurse who would be looking after Joe, Phoebe, one of the other patients, came back from the education centre. What struck me immediately was that she could have been Joe's twin sister. She was a very attractive girl, although gaunt and extremely thin, she spoke very quietly and floated around as though in a trance. I wondered if she and Joe were having similar thoughts and feelings, and if The Great Barn would be able to help them both to overcome their fears and anxieties or whatever was causing this self-starvation. She had been admitted the previous Tuesday and so was still in the early stages of settling in but she seemed at ease with her surroundings, another positive sign. As she was still in the early stages of her re-feeding programme she was not allowed to go home for the weekend, so she would be company for Joe on his first weekend.

Then Joe's nurse arrived. She introduced herself as Fiona Ward, but told Joe that most of the other patients called her Fifi. She took us upstairs so that Joe could unpack his things. Joe had been allocated a spacious yellow corner room and it took all of two minutes to unpack his bag, and distribute his things around the room. With his get well cards, several family photos and several of Joe's school team photos (football, cricket and rugby) on display I felt that this could be a haven for Joe when he was feeling down or homesick. A small comfort knowing that we would shortly be leaving him on his own in this strange place, but a comfort nonetheless. Fiona suggested to Joe he might like to put his slippers on, and I caught James's eye across the room. Was this going to trigger a tantrum from Joe or perhaps open the floodgates to his tears of anxiety? He wasn't used to wearing slippers at home and had already indicated to me that he didn't want to wear them when he was at the adolescent unit because he thought the other teenagers would laugh at him. I had explained that I thought everyone would wear slippers, but he hadn't believed me. Surprisingly there was no tantrum at this stage. Joe calmly asked if he had to, to which Fiona replied that she thought it would be a good idea, especially as the floor downstairs had just been cleaned and could be slippery. Joe dutifully obliged, the first house rule had been established, the first hurdle had been stepped over without incident.

What happens at an adolescent unit?

Back downstairs there were the inevitable forms to fill in and consent forms to sign, and Fiona was happy to answer all our initial questions and chat about what Joe's first few weeks at The Great Barn would involve.

In this session we were all given a booklet providing essential and useful information for young people admitted to The Great Barn and their families or guardians. Among other things it described the daily routine, the rules, the staff and what to do if things go wrong. The unit is operated by the local Community Health Care Trust (i.e. part of the NHS) and has live-in space for ten young people who are experiencing some emotional, personal or family difficulties, within the age range of 11 to 17 years. Everyone is encouraged to participate in the day-to-day running of the unit and to share responsibility for domestic duties. The aim is for each patient to stay as short a time as possible before being reintegrated back into his or her normal family and school routine. We were soon to discover that whilst some patients might be admitted for a few weeks, others might stay for many months, depending on the problems they were having and the success of their treatment. When Joe was admitted, there were three other patients with eating disorders, all of who were girls; there was one other boy, who was 17 years old and had behavioural problems. The turnover of patients was quite high, and during Joe's stay he would meet many teenagers, all with different issues that a stay in The Great Barn would help them resolve. Fiona was very open and honest and suggested that Joe would be staying for at least three or four months, slightly longer than I had thought at first, but Joe seemed unfazed by this.

Fiona explained that each patient has an individual therapeutic programme consisting of individual and group therapy and family work. The appropriate programme for Joe would be worked out once he had settled in and was a little stronger. Families are expected to be actively involved in the therapeutic programme, this may involve structured Family Therapy sessions, informal meetings or family mealtimes.

Patients have access to day services and education at a day centre about half a mile from The Great Barn. The day centre operates Monday to Friday, but education is only provided in school term time. Joe would not be expected to participate in the education sessions until he was much stronger, but he would go to the day centre with the other patients. At the beginning he would spend most of his time resting and seeing the therapists and doctors.

The unit also organises a wide range of activities and days out, particularly in the school holidays. Joe would not be allowed to participate in these until he had reached a healthy weight.

Most patients go home for weekends and spend more time at home in the school holidays. However patients in the early stage of re-feeding have to stay on the unit full time to start with. Joe would not be allowed home until he had reached a more healthy weight.

Joe's re-feeding programme would be put together by a dietician specialising in eating disorders. Fiona explained that Joe would be given very small meals to start with, as they didn't want to overburden his weak heart. The size of his meals would be built up gradually over the course of the next few weeks and then we should start to see a healthy weight gain. A target weight would be established that would be appropriate for Joe's age and height.

There are special meal guidelines for children with eating disorders. Joe would have to eat at the assisted re-feeding table, which is in the same room, but separate from the main dining table for the other patients. The re-feeding table is assisted by at least two members of staff. One member of staff sits at the table throughout the meal and provides support and encouragement to the patients. The other member of staff takes things to and from the kitchen and serves up the meal. Everyone has to sit at the table until the last person has finished. The idea is that all the children with eating disorders support each other through each meal. There are set maximum times for each meal.

Each patient is allocated a case manager and a key worker. Fiona was to be Joe's case manager and she would have overall responsibility for Joe during his stay. Joe's key worker was to be a lady called Amanda, who would help Joe settle in, explaining the daily routine, expectations of patients during their stay and the rules.

Each patient has an 'action plan'. This is a written document put together by the patient and his care team. It aims to provide a framework so that each patient can make the best use of his/her time in the unit. It is updated regularly, and the patient should always have an updated copy.

The staff on the unit, and at the associated day centre, have a wide range of experience and include doctors, nurses, teachers, therapists and psychologists. In addition each patient has a consultant psychiatrist who is responsible for the overall care. In Joe's case this was Dr Cornwall. All the staff work closely together and have regular meetings to discuss the best ways of helping each patient. At key stages in the patient's treatment programme a professionals' meeting is held. This includes the patient's medical and education team at The Great Barn, and representatives from the patient's community medical team, GP and school and his parents or guardians.

Fiona then spoke briefly about staff observation of new patients. For obvious reasons new patients are observed very closely for the first few days, in order to assess their frame of mind and to ensure they are settling in. There are several levels of observation. Level four is constant supervision by a member of staff and Joe should expect to be under this level at least for his meal and rest times. Under level three the patient's whereabouts is checked every fifteen minutes. To start with Joe would be under level three supervision outside of meal and rest times, including through the night. If Joe was non-compliant, or his behaviour was deemed to be unacceptable at any time he would be reprimanded and possibly moved on to level four supervision. After a period of time Joe's level of supervision would be reduced to levels two and one, which were more at the discretion of the staff on duty. Until that time Joe would not be allowed to go upstairs or outside without being accompanied by a member of staff.

A carers' support group meets once a month so that parents/guardians can meet together with staff and discuss their concerns and views about having a family member in the unit.

The rules of the unit are pretty basic. No violent or aggressive behaviour, no drugs, no sex, no racist or sexist behaviour and a reasonable attempt to take part in the programme. Non-compliance could lead to suspension from the unit.

Having run through all these issues, Fiona gently explained to Joe that the first few days might not be that easy. He might feel homesick, sad or upset and angry. He might question why his parents had placed him here. He might find it difficult if some of the other young people got upset or angry. She explained that most patients have some or all of these feelings to start with. However, in the end most patients settle in and learn to cope with their problems and sort out their difficulties. Most patients benefit enormously from their stay and in the end most have fun and enjoy themselves as well. It was clear that life was going to be very regimented, but it was also clear that this was what Joe needed in order to help him back on the road to recovery. Fiona had fully explained what life at The Great Barn would be like, but it was clear that for at least the first few weeks Joe would not be allowed to participate in very much. I wondered how they were going to keep Joe occupied over this period.

By this stage Joe looked exhausted and it was time for us to say goodbye, Joe needed to see Dr Cornwall, settle in and have his first meal. Fiona suggested we return around 7.30 that evening, giving Joe plenty of time to recover from the inevitable trauma of having to sit down and eat with complete strangers.

Mummy, please take me home – I promise I'll eat

When we returned I was fully expecting tears, anger and pleading to come home, but nothing could have prepared me for the extent of Joe's distress. He leapt up off the sofa and rushed into my arms, his eyes were already very red and swollen from previous sobbing, and he proceeded to beg and plead to be given one more chance to come home. I had to be strong. Everything I had read about the treatment of anorexics had told me this but I felt like my heart was being ripped in two. All my motherly instincts were telling me to scoop this fragile sick child up in my arms and whisk him back to the safety and security of his home, but I knew I had to totally suppress these feelings and appear calm on the surface for Joe's sake. I firmly explained to Joe that we couldn't take him home and that we all knew that this was the best place for him to be. Joe however was so distressed that my words fell on deaf ears. Over and over again he kept repeating the same pleas: "Mummy, Mummy please give me one more chance. I promise I will eat and drink anything you want me to if you let me come home. If you leave me here I won't eat or drink anything. I don't care if I die." He carried on sobbing and sobbing, begging and pleading for about half an hour, which seemed like an eternity, before pure exhaustion took over and he became a crumpled dishevelled heap in my arms. Eventually Joe withdrew completely, humming to himself so he couldn't hear what I was saying. The words you have to be cruel to be kind have never rung truer in my ears.

Reward for good behaviour

When Joe had calmed down we met with Fiona who explained that Joe had been very good at eating his first, albeit tiny, meal but that he was really struggling with drinking. Fiona suggested that in order to help Joe settle in it might be better if we didn't visit the next day. Fiona said she would call, and if Joe had a really good day perhaps we could visit in the evening, but more than likely she would recommend we visit on Sunday.

Walking away was one of the hardest things I have ever had to do. Once we were back in the car I succumbed to my emotions and sobbed most of the way home. That night seemed to drag on for eternity. I certainly felt relieved that Joe was now in very safe hands, but my mind was tormented by the fact that

Joe must feel I had deserted him and left him with complete strangers who were forcing him to do things that he couldn't do for me.

The next day Tom was going off on the school ski trip. It couldn't have been more perfect timing. We could get Joe settled in without having to worry about keeping Tom occupied at home. I waved goodbye to Tom as the coach left at 6 am and then returned home to count the minutes until I could ring The Great Barn.

The battle begins

By 9.30 am I could hold on no longer. The news was not good. Fiona explained to me that having gone to bed early and slept quite well Joe was in defiant mood, and was refusing to eat or drink unless his family could come and bring him home. He had been sent back to bed under constant supervision of a nurse and was told that a doctor would be coming to see him mid-morning to assess how long he could go without fluids before being transferred over to the main hospital to be rehydrated with an IV drip. I could immediately feel the panic rise up inside me. Would Joe lose his place at The Great Barn that we had fought so hard for because of his stubbornness? As always Fiona was the voice of calm and rational thought. Of course he would not lose his place and if necessary they would send him over to the hospital on more than one occasion for rehydration. Fiona did request, though, that if this were to happen that we would continue to stay away, explaining that if we visited him in hospital he would feel he had won a victory. I heard myself saying that if Fiona felt we should stay away for weeks on end we would do that, but my heart was still aching for me to jump in the car and rush over to answer my child's call for help. I have heard and read about many instances where parents have severely hindered their child's progress by being overly protective and ignoring the professional staff's request to stay away if the child is refusing to comply with the prescribed treatment regime or action plan. The child learns very quickly that he or she can control his or her parent's behaviour, and this can have devastating long-term effects on the rest of the family including, of course, siblings. Having absorbed this depressing news and having relayed it to my husband and ex husband, I announced that I was going to go and catch up with one of my girlfriends.

Friends are so important

I cannot stress how important friends are at a time like this. The family becomes so immersed in the anorexic world that the outside world seems far away. Friends can really help to keep your feet on the ground, give you a welcome break from the highly charged family situation, and help keep some sort of normality in your life. I went to see Monica, who was not only a very good friend, but also the mum's representative for Joe's class at school. Talking to Monica for the next two hours was akin to having a verbal massage. She reassured me that I was doing all the right things and sympathised with the agony we must be going through. Two cups of tea and much discussion later we were on to much more light hearted topics and I felt normality returning to my mind albeit for a short period of time. I gave Monica a letter to distribute to all the other mums in the class. Monica had been inundated with calls enquiring after Joe. Monica was not sure how much to give away, so the easiest thing was for me to write a letter stating all the facts. It seems that there is still a fear of eating disorders and for some it is a taboo subject.

My letter read as follows:

Dear Class Mums,

Sorry for the impersonal address but I am snatching a moment between sleep and hospital to put this update down on paper, and Monica has very kindly offered to circulate it to you.

First I would like to thank you all profusely for all your kind messages in recent weeks and the beautiful flowers. We feel so lucky to be surrounded by such a fantastic network of mums and boys, I imagine many families in our situation would feel incredibly isolated! Most importantly Joe has gone into hospital in the knowledge that all the boys in his class are gunning for him and he takes great comfort in having all the lovely class cards on display in his bedroom (Mr Dunston has of course been fantastic in co-ordinating this).

As you have all observed, Joe's health has deteriorated dramatically over the last couple of months. We have had every medical examination under the sun done and (thank goodness) these all proved negative. The initial psychiatric analysis has diagnosed 'severe anorexia nervosa', which means he has lost 25% of his body weight, and in Joe's case it has been very quick. There is no simple explanation (could be social, chemical, biological, physiological or a combination of all of these) and sometimes the trigger is totally irrelevant to the recovery. Having read a few books and talked to the psychiatrist, it is evident that this condition is unusual but not unheard of in 12-year-old boys. Sufferers are often very talented and bright and come from a very wide variety of backgrounds. It is a vicious disease in that the more you lose your weight and strength, the more your body's defences fall down, and the more susceptible you are to low self-esteem, and obsessive behaviour. On a brighter note once you regain weight these tendencies tend to reverse very quickly.

Joe is extremely fortunate to have been admitted to a unit called The Great Barn which specialises in treating children aged 11 to 17 with a wide range of problems (eating disorders, emotional, behavioural etc). It is a lovely spacious house with very caring and qualified staff, and we believe it is the perfect place for Joe to be in his recovery phase. He is likely to be there for several months. It will probably take a week or so for him to settle in, but after that Joe would love to have visits from his school friends. Meanwhile his address is attached if anyone wants to send him cards/letters/postcards etc. Once Joe is fit to have visitors we will let you know, and if you and/or your son would like to visit, please let Monica or me know and we will let you know when it is possible.

Thanks again for all your kind thoughts and support throughout this time.

Breaking Joe's will

Monica was doing a fantastic job of lifting my spirits, although I was still feeling very nervy and when my mobile rang I immediately assumed it would be further bad news of Joe's behaviour or progress. I couldn't have been more wrong. It was Fiona telling me that Joe had agreed to eat and drink. She relayed the process that they had gone through before Joe finally relented.

Having refused any fluids at breakfast and being sent back to bed, Joe had tried to manipulate the situation by saying that he would eat and drink if his parents could come and sit with him. When this didn't work, he had changed his tune and stated that he didn't care if he never saw his parents again, he would still not be able to drink. Fiona had explained to him that there would be no bargaining and that he could not go home until he was well. At this point Joe, obviously in defiant mood, had said he didn't care if he had to go back to hospital for IV fluids, he simply could not drink orally. Fiona had then called the duty doctor, to come and assess how long Joe should be left with no fluid intake before being readmitted to hospital. An hour later Joe had asked the nurse supervising him to fetch Fiona. Once again he had tried to bargain with Fiona by suggesting he would only eat and drink if his parents could come and sit with him, but obviously this was not acceptable to Fiona. Fiona gave him the clear message that at The Great Barn the staff were in control, not the anorexia. She told him that if he ate his breakfast and his lunch, and drank his drinks, she would call us and get us to visit in the afternoon. Fiona told Joe that she was keeping us updated. We had sent our love, wanted to visit and were missing him, but we had already agreed with her that all the time he was being non-compliant we would stay away.

When Fiona called me Joe had had his breakfast and a drink, and so as long as he did the same at lunchtime we could visit at 3 pm. I felt so much better when I finally left Monica's and returned home in much better spirits to report the good news.

Mummy I'll die if you don't take me home

We arrived at The Great Barn at 3 pm to find Joe is very sombre mood, almost in a trance, and quite uncommunicative. It seemed as if his spirit had been broken, which I guess in effect it had. We persuaded him to have a game of pool and he reluctantly shuffled into the poolroom. After a couple of shots I could see he was about to crack and sure enough a few minutes later the floodgates opened and he was once again begging me to take him home. "Mummy, I hate it here, I promise I'll eat and drink if you take me home. There is no one here like me or for me to talk to. I cannot stay here more than a week. If you leave me here I'm going to die, I'll jump out of my bedroom window; you just have to take me home. It doesn't matter if I die at home because if I stay here I am definitely going to die. You don't believe me but I promise you I am going to commit suicide." He ranted and raved for several minutes whilst two of the staff on duty, Roger and Mandy, tried to calm him and explain to him that if he carried on being so upset then they would have to ask us to leave. Needless to say my heart was breaking into a thousand pieces while this was all going on. My maternal instinct to bundle him up and take him home was having a huge fight with my head, which knew he was in the best place to ensure a full recovery.

Re-feeding – don't rush it

Joe managed to calm himself enough for us to proceed to the library to discuss his action plan with Mandy. This had been put together by Fiona and set out what Joe would be expected to achieve over the next few days. He would continue to be given tiny meals (quarter portions) for the next couple of days, and should have an hour bed-rest after each meal. Joe asked why he was being given such tiny portions when he could manage more and Mandy explained that this was to avoid 're-feeding syndrome', a potentially fatal condition caused by the body's reaction to suddenly being given more food to digest. I had had no idea how serious this could be. If Joe had agreed to eat more at home, I potentially could have killed him by building back up too quickly. Another good reason for Joe to stay put. Joe was amazingly calm and coherent as we went through the action plan. He seemed to understand why things should be taken slowly and that he would be here for a while. We all signed the action plan and Mandy left us to spend some more time with Joe.

Joe agreed to play a game of Cluedo, but as soon as I unpacked it he burst into tears and started ranting and raving once more. I can only say that while it is never ever going to be easy to see your child in such a distressed state it does become easier to cope with and you build up a kind of immunity. Nonetheless when we left Joe we all felt totally exhausted and emotionally drained. Just before we left a girl called Rebecca arrived and started chatting to Joe about football. I was mightily relieved, she seemed to be a very pleasant girl and whilst Joe was not being terribly interactive, he was certainly listening to her comments. In fact as we got into the car Roger rushed out to tell us that Joe was now chatting happily with Rebecca, so we left on a brighter note.

Key points from Joe's first action plan

Problem/need:

- Joe has difficulty eating and an unhealthy low weight for his age.
- Joe needs an assessment of his functioning and needs support settling in to The Great Barn.

Aims/outcomes:

- Joe will comply with the re-feeding programme.
- Joe will have a general assessment of his functioning and receive support from the staff physically and psychologically.

Nursing interventions:

- Joe will be nursed on level three generally, and level four for bed-rest, which will be 30 minutes after snacks and one hour after main meals. Joe to have escort outside The Great Barn with transport as necessary by car. Joe will have no access upstairs other than for rests and minimal activity generally.

- Joe will comply with the re-feeding programme. He is allowed three dislikes which he will not be asked to eat. They are tomatoes, eggs on their own and cheesecake. There will be consequences for non-compliance, for example, no visits from family. Staff will support Joe if he has difficulties. Bed-rest may be extended by shift co-ordinator.

- Joe's physical observations to be taken during each shift and more often if necessary. Staff will observe for any symptoms of Re-feeding Syndrome.

- Joe will be weighed weekly.

- Nurse to give medication if prescribed.

- Assessment framework to be completed each shift as appropriate.

(This documents Joe's appearance, mood, thought processes, social interaction etc.)

- Care team or shift co-ordinator to liaise regularly with family and Multi Disciplinary Team, (MDT, which includes all professional members, involved in Joe's care).

On Sunday Joe complied fully with his re-feeding programme and we visited in the afternoon. Joe was very subdued and uncommunicative for the first half-hour and I was fully expecting him to, once again, start begging and pleading to come home. However, he suddenly seemed to perk up and started chatting happily about the football. He was very clearly in full control of the TV remote (typical male) and navigated his way expertly from sports programme to teletext and back again. His snack time was 3.30 pm, and after drinking his 150 ml glass of cold milk, he had to return to the sofa for his half-hour rest. This was supervised by one of the staff. Joe made the mistake of getting up after 15 minutes to come and sit next to me, but was immediately reprimanded, albeit gently, for making such a move. The rules were very strict: there should be no moving around whatsoever in the rest period.

Mummy, they keep you here too long

Joe had come to sit with me because he wanted to address the issue of how much weight he would be expected to put on. I simply didn't have an answer for this question as the dietician had not yet come up with a target weight for Joe. This would be done over the next few days. Joe said he knew that he had to put quite a lot of weight back on to be healthy, but was clearly worried that he might be forced to put too much weight on. At this stage he hadn't realised that many of the patients had illnesses other than eating disorders.

"Mummy, they keep you here too long, some of the other patients are quite chubby." I explained to Joe that many of the patients had problems, which were not related to food, but that for reasons of confidentiality, the staff could not discuss other patient's illnesses openly. I felt sure that once Joe got to know the other patients better, he would find out what problems they were having.

Strict daily routine

The next time we visited, Joe had had his first day at the day centre and was clearly feeling more settled. He described his daily routine, Monday to Friday, as it had been set out by his care team, for the first two weeks:

Rise at 7.30 am, breakfast at 8 am.

To start with Joe has a quarter portion (half a shredded wheat with milk, half a piece of toast with crunchy peanut butter, 200 ml orange juice). This will increase to half portions after a few days and then to full portions by the end of the second week. Joe manages to eat quickly from the beginning, but this is quite unusual for the newly admitted anorexics. He is expected to wait for any fellow patients on the assisted re-feeding table, as part of the treatment process is learning to be supportive to those around you. All food must be consumed. The maximum time allowed for breakfast is stated as half an hour. After breakfast Joe has to have an hour bed-rest supervised by one of the care team. During this time he is not allowed to move, and occupies himself by reading, listening to his tapes, playing cards or chatting to the care nurse. If non-compliance is an issue during a meal or snack time, then 15 minutes can be added to the rest period.

Community Group is at 9.30 am. All the young people and staff meet to talk about what's happening on the unit, to share feelings and to sort out problems. This is the patients' chance to air any concerns that they have. Sometimes nobody speaks for half an hour but apparently the current group, including Joe, is quite lively. Joe came to quite enjoy these meetings.

After the Community Group, the formal day programme starts. All the staff and patients move to the day centre, which is about half a mile from The Great Barn. The physically fit children walk, whilst those patients like Joe and Phoebe, who are very weak or on early re-feeding, are driven. Everyone arrives between 10 am and 10.30 am. There are also some day-patients attending the unit. During term time most of the patients attend some lessons, although it was several weeks before Joe was strong enough to join in with education. In the school holidays, much of the day is spent playing games. There is also a range of activities and therapies, as well as medical assessments.

At 11 am Joe has a snack (glass of milk) followed by 30 minutes supervised rest on the sofa. Joe has to wait until any fellow patients have finished their snack before moving to the rest area. The maximum snack time is stated as 15 minutes.

Lunch is at 12.30 pm. As at The Great Barn, Joe eats at the assisted re-feeding table and has to wait for any fellow patients to finish, before moving to the rest area. The maximum stated time for the first course is 45 minutes, and 15 minutes for the second course. Joe states that the cook at the education centre is excellent. Joe reported that on his first day he had a delicious chicken in sauce with rice and he was disappointed that he was only allowed a quarter portion. Joe also had a glass of milk and then another hour of supervised rest on the sofa.

After lunch there are more activities. On his first day Joe saw Dr Cornwall, and she rang me immediately after this session to report how pleased she was with his progress. She felt his anxiety levels had dropped dramatically and she did not feel he needed any medication, such as anti-depressants, at this time. I was very relieved, as we wanted to avoid any drug interaction for my son, if at all possible.

At 3.30 pm Joe has another snack (glass of milk), followed by 30 minutes supervised rest on the sofa.

From 4 pm onwards everyone drifts back to The Great Barn. From 4 pm to 6 pm is free time, unless you have an individual therapy session with one of the care staff.

Dinner is at 6 pm. As for the other meals, to start with Joe has just a quarter portion. Today was a quarter of a jacket potato with a tiny piece of homemade pizza and a glass of milk. The maximum stated times are the same as for lunch. This is followed by an hour of supervised bed-rest.

Visiting is 6.30 pm to 8.30 pm on Monday, Wednesday and Friday. On Tuesday and Thursday evenings, group activities and games are arranged by the staff. Letters and telephone calls are encouraged, both from patients and to patients. For practical reasons it is suggested that telephone calls should be made between 4 pm and 8 pm.

At 8.30 pm Joe has a final snack (glass of milk) followed by 30 minutes supervised bed-rest.

Bedtime for 14 year olds and under is 9.30 pm and lights out by 10 pm. Bedtime for over 14 year olds is 10 pm, with lights out by 10.30 pm.

Joe seemed quite happy now that he knew what his daily routine would be during the week. He clearly found time spent at the day centre much more interesting than time spent at The Great Barn. It was a welcome change of scenery and there were more things going on. What struck me about Joe's routine was how much time he was expected to sit at the re-feeding table and then resting. If the maximum mealtimes were taken by the other patients then Joe would effectively be sitting still or lying down for nearly seven hours each day. The rest of the time Joe had to be as inactive as possible. He was reprimanded if he showed the slightest signs of activity such as skipping across a room rather than walking. I wondered how long Joe would put up with this incredibly strict regime.

The first major setback

Before we could find out Joe suffered his first major setback. On Joe's sixth day at The Great Barn the phone rang at 10.30 am. It was Trevor, one of the care workers at The Great Barn. My heart sank as he explained that Joe had been taken by ambulance to the local hospital. Joe had been totally compliant with his eating and rest regime, but had woken up feeling very poorly. His temperature had dropped, he felt dizzy and the care staff were concerned that his blood pressure and pulse were still way too low. As a precaution they had called an ambulance, so that Joe could be given proper emergency care if his condition deteriorated any further. Trevor explained that Joe was understandably extremely upset at this development and that we should go straight to the hospital.

When we caught up with Joe in the paediatric ward I was relieved to see he looked quite calm. Trevor was sitting with him and they seemed to be having some banter about football. The next hour was taken up with the inevitable questions from several different doctors and nurses, and lots of form filling. By this stage Steve had taken over from Trevor in chatting to Joe about football. Then the doctors and nurses suddenly seemed to disappear all at once. Joe immediately took the opportunity to vent his anger at what seemed to him to be a massive setback:

"It's not fair. You all promised me that if I ate and drank everything put in front of me I wouldn't have to come back to hospital. How can I trust anyone? You are all liars. Now they are going to keep me locked up for longer. I know they are."

By this stage he was sobbing and our assurances that this was just a precautionary visit to hospital to check things out, fell on deaf ears. I explained to Joe that we were really pleased with the progress he was making, but that he had to understand that he was still very poorly and inevitably things would have to be taken one small step at a time. At this point Joe's case manager Fiona Ward arrived. She endorsed everything that I had said and promised Joe that this didn't mean an extended stay at The Great Barn. Joe, however, was not in a receptive mood. His frustrations were running high and he was alternately upset and angry. He told the senior registrar in no uncertain terms that he thought the doctors and nurses were a complete waste of time and that none of them knew what they were doing. Luckily she took it in good spirit, and having now vented his anger at several different people Joe seemed to calm down a little. Steve managed to get Joe back onto the subject of football, and within a few minutes Joe was smiling again.

Fiona took the opportunity to take me aside. It wasn't just Joe's temperature, pulse and blood pressure that they were worried about. Joe's blood test from the previous day had shown dangerously high levels of creatin and urea. This indicated that Joe was still seriously dehydrated. Fiona agreed with me that this was puzzling. Joe had three nights on a drip at the first hospital and for the last four days had been drinking plenty of fluid at The Great Barn, under tight supervision. My fears that Joe might have done permanent damage to his internal organs resurfaced. Fiona didn't say as much, but I was under the impression that she was worried too. It is highly unusual for a child to get dehydrated again so quickly. Another blood test was urgently needed, so poor Joe had to endure yet more needles. This did nothing to improve his general state of mind.

Thankfully our fears were unfounded. The blood tests were carried out in record time and showed that Joe was still dehydrated, but only mildly so. It was decided, much to Joe's relief, that he didn't need to have a drip overnight, but that he should stay in hospital for observation. Joe also had an ECG, which confirmed that his heart was beating normally, albeit a little slow.

The one positive sign that came out of this hospital stay was Joe's determination to stick to his re-feeding plan. At the appropriate times he would tell me it was time for his snack or next meal. Obviously we couldn't be as regimented in the portion sizes as they were at The Great Barn, but Joe had a very clear idea of how much he should be eating and drinking and it seemed to be a sensible amount to me. Joe was still petrified of getting fat, but he definitely wanted to beat this strange illness and get back to normality as quickly as possible.

At peace with the world

Joe was keen to get back to The Great Barn as soon as possible. He didn't plead with me to take him straight home, but simply stated that he wanted to get on with his treatment so that he could come home as soon as possible. Inevitably we had to hang around the hospital for hours so that further checks could be made, and the registrar could formally discharge Joe. Because it was such a nice day I asked one of the nurses if I could take Joe for a short walk outside. She agreed. It was the first time Joe had been outside for a walk since being admitted to The Great Barn. The sun warmed our faces and Joe linked his arm with mine. He still shuffled like an old man, but not nearly as badly as he had done two weeks before. He said very little, but was at peace with the world. I hoped this feeling would last, but realistically I knew that Rex was still lurking in his head and could pounce at any moment.

We returned to The Great Barn late morning. The teenage girls, who were busy planning a dance show, gave Joe a rapturous welcome. Joe was clearly delighted to be back and we left him in high spirits, chuckling at the girls' antics.

The nightmare of long meals and bed-rest

Within a couple of days of being back at The Great Barn Joe started to get very frustrated about the long meals and bed-rest. He rang me to vent his fury. One of the other patients, Phoebe, was struggling to finish her meals in the allotted maximum time. Joe was still on half portions and was having milk rather than puddings. He was managing to eat at a normal rate and so was finishing most meals in five to ten minutes. Phoebe had just moved onto full portions and was struggling to eat her meal in the allotted maximum times. Joe claimed that sometimes he had to sit with Phoebe for more than an hour at mealtimes and half an hour at snack times (i.e. the staff were not being strict about the maximum allowed times). Then he was taken to his room for an hour supervised bed-rest, while Phoebe was allowed to sit on the sofa in the lounge for her rest. Phoebe could chat to the other patients and watch television, while Joe was locked in his room. I did a quick mental calculation and realised that under this scenario Joe had to sit at the re-feeding table and lie on his bed for up to eight hours during the day. No wonder he was angry. I tried to explain to Joe that there was very good reason why he needed to rest after his meals. He was still very poorly, but things would improve in time if he stuck to the regime. Joe reluctantly took this on board, but was clearly very upset. Once again I said I would discuss this issue with Fiona. I felt totally inadequate as I said goodbye and put the phone down.

At 9.30 pm I rang Fiona. As always I apologised for bothering her. As always she indicated this was no problem. I addressed the issue of Joe having to sit so long to wait for Phoebe. I explained that we all understood the special eating guidelines, but Joe felt he was having to sit for longer than the allotted maximum times at each meal. This is what was making Joe so angry. I also explained that we all understood why Joe still needed to rest on his bed, but that it wasn't easy for a 12-year-old boy to accept. Joe felt left out of the general activity downstairs when he was confined to his bedroom. Fiona agreed that this was difficult and promised to reassure Joe that it wouldn't be forever. In addition she said she would remind both Joe and Phoebe of the maximum mealtimes and ask the staff supervising the meals to try and stick to these times.

I then addressed the fact that Joe felt Fiona was always too busy to talk to him and that he didn't feel so comfortable talking to other members of staff. Fiona replied that it was very common for children to cling to one member of staff early on in their stay, but that they soon learned to discuss any anxieties with other members of staff. She also said it was unfortunate that Joe's arrival had coincided with a holiday period, as the normally strict routine was a lot more haphazard.

So far so good

We ended the conversation on a brighter note. Fiona was really pleased that Joe had settled back in so well after his brief visit to the local hospital. She told me that he was a popular addition to The Great Barn, that he was chatty and polite, both with his peers and the staff. She felt that this first week had progressed extremely well. I was comforted by this phone call and I hoped that Joe would be similarly comforted by a follow up discussion with Fiona.

Bad Friday

The next day was Good Friday. Most of the patients had gone home for the Easter weekend. Joe rang me mid-morning in floods of tears. He had only just finished his bed-rest after breakfast, which had gone on for much longer than half an hour. Now it was already his snack time. He didn't think he could bear it any longer. I could understand why Joe was so upset and I felt angry that the meals were still being allowed to go on indefinitely. When I visited Joe later that day I had some strong words for Richard, the care nurse on duty.

The first few weeks are really tough

Richard explained that the first few weeks in a residential unit are tough for most patients, but particularly for a 12-year-old boy like Joe, who desperately wants to be normal and who desperately wants to go home. In addition because Joe was so frail they had to err on the side of caution. Joe's pulse rate and blood pressure were still abnormally low and, until they rose to a more steady and normal rate, it made sense to keep him on bed-rest after his meals. At this stage it was too early to be making any promises. If they made a promise that Joe would be off bed-rest in two weeks but then had to change their minds, Joe would be even angrier.

Richard also told me that it was very common for children to ring their parents every day for the first few weeks in floods of tears. They would say the staff were being unfair, that the patients were horrible and that nobody understands them. Like me, most parents would then ring the staff office to relay their child's distress. More often than not, by this stage the child in question would be back happily playing with their peers or watching television. Richard reassured me that Joe was doing really well, and his initial feelings of anger and frustration were entirely normal. It was more than likely that Joe would find the first few weeks extremely difficult, but after that things should start to improve dramatically.

Sure enough the next two weeks followed a similar pattern. It was as if the clock had stopped. Joe was fully compliant with his re-feeding programme, but seemed to be making little progress. He continued to have to endure endless mealtimes and bed-rest and he became very angry and upset almost on a daily basis. The Easter weekend was particularly difficult because most of the patients had gone home and there was only a skeleton staff on duty. There was very little to distract Joe from his anger and frustration.

Looking forward

On day 12, which was just after the Easter weekend, Steve, James and I had a very useful meeting with Dr Cornwall. With lots of temporary staff being on duty over the Easter break we felt that Joe had been given some very confusing messages and that in general communication between the family and Joe's care team had broken down. In the meeting Dr Cornwall brought us fully up to date on her views on Joe's progress. Whilst she couldn't make any tangible promises she reiterated the original view from Fiona that Joe would be at The Great Barn for three to four months. Dr Cornwall had seen Joe that morning and whilst she had explained to Joe that he was still very poorly and should not do any exercise for the foreseeable future, she had agreed to his request to go to the Tottenham/West Ham match with his dad on April 13th. It would be several more weeks before he would be allowed home for visits, but at least this outing was something for Joe to look forward to and a step in the right direction. Dr Cornwall also told us that in view of the fact that Joe was being totally compliant with his re-feeding programme and the boundaries set out in his action plan, Joe's care team had decided to reduce his general observation level from three to level two. This was another sign of good progress being made, although Joe might not appreciate it as much as being allowed to go to the football match. This change to observation levels would be noted in Joe's action plan.

I asked Dr Cornwall to give us her opinion of Joe's physical condition. She indicated that she felt Joe was still extremely fragile which was why they had to be so strict about his eating programme and his bed-rest. His pulse was averaging 45; sometimes creeping up to 50, but this was still too low. The normal range for a boy his age would be 60 to 80. His blood pressure was also too low. In the last week it had ranged from 95/29 to 70/40. Such a wide variation is not unusual, but Dr Cornwall indicated she would be much happier if it stabilised at around 100/80. She also explained that they would continue to monitor his blood very carefully. The signs so far were good and with the exception of the one set of blood tests at the hospital, which had indicated that Joe was very dehydrated, Joe's blood test results had been within the normal range. However, Dr Cornwall did say that if Joe had carried on his self-starvation his kidneys would have become damaged very quickly.

After our meeting we visited Joe for a short while. He seemed reasonably relaxed although he was still frustrated at not being able to do any exercise or have any privacy in his room. On the other hand he was clearly delighted that he was to be allowed to go to the football match in ten days' time.

The first parents/carers' meeting

We all visited that evening. Steve and his wife Jessica arrived first with Tom and Tom's two younger half siblings. James and I arrived in time to see Joe briefly before attending our first parent/carers meeting. These meetings occur once a month and are designed for parents and carers of the patients to meet each other. Two members of staff are present to begin with to give parents the opportunity to ask questions and express any concerns. Then the parents are left to talk among themselves. It was good to meet some of the other parents. Some wanted to be very much involved in their child's treatment and, like us, were constantly asking the staff questions about their child's progress. Others were much more hands off and were happy to leave their child in the capable hands of the staff at The Great Barn.

The patients at The Great Barn have a wide variety of illnesses and come from a wide range of backgrounds.

Naturally we ended up talking to the parents of two anorexic girls who had been at The Great Barn for several months already. They had very similar stories to tell. Both families had found it extremely difficult when the girls had been allowed home. They explained that the girls became very nervous and agitated when they left the restrictive boundaries of The Great Barn for the first time. It became even more difficult once the girls were allowed to have meals at home and that that is when the battle against anorexia really begins. Can your child manage to eat a proper meal in a normal family environment? At The Great Barn they have no choice. They sit at the re-feeding table supervised by two members of staff and there is the peer pressure of seeing other patients with the same illness eating their meals without a fuss. It is a very different scenario at home and both sets of parents relayed stories of the various battles they had had and the tricks that the girls had played to try to avoid eating. It was all exactly as described in the books I had read. For example, the girls were expert at hiding food, they drank litres of water to ensure the scales showed a respectable weight and they secretly exercised. Emma, who had been at The Great Barn for seven months, had managed to fool her parents that she was eating enough to maintain her weight over the Christmas holidays. In fact she had been drinking gallons of water before her weighing sessions. When she returned to The Great Barn and her fluid intake was restricted to a more normal level, it was discovered she had managed to lose 8 lbs in just ten days. At this stage she had been at The Great Barn for four months, so this was quite a major setback.

Both sets of parents also said that their daughters did not want to get better. They wanted to stay thin, they felt secure at The Great Barn and they did not want to go back to school. I hoped Joe would be different. He had already said that he wanted to get better. He certainly didn't want to put on too much weight, but he knew he needed to put on weight to play sport. He had lost weight in the first place so that he would be better at sport and now had defeated his objective by making himself very sick indeed. On balance the meeting increased my nervousness about the months ahead, but I was hanging on to the hope that the lure of sport would help Joe to overcome this complicated illness.

Joe's first weekly review

After the carers' meeting, Amanda talked James, Steve and me through Joe's first proper weekly review. These occurred every Wednesday and the patients were often very nervous about them. Each patient's consultant, case manager and key worker would meet to discuss his or her progress. Those with eating disorders would be weighed and decisions would be made about such things as observation levels, bed-rest, appropriate activity levels, home visits etc. Joe had missed his review meeting the previous week because he had been rushed back into hospital, so this was a big day for him.

Joe's weight had increased to 33 kg. This was fantastic news. Whilst The Great Barn did not have specific weight gain targets each week, I had read that other treatment centres did. An increase of 1 kg per week seemed to be what was generally accepted as reasonable. Despite Joe's trip back into hospital he had put on nearly 2 kg in just under two weeks. Amanda talked us through all the decisions from this week's review. Basically nothing had changed for Joe in terms of bed-rest and re-feeding, but the main positive point was that Joe could work towards going to the football match with his dad in two weeks' time.

Joe's case manager also wrote several pages of notes following each review meeting. These were not shared with the family, but we have had access to them since Joe's recovery. At times during Joe's stay it was very difficult for us as a family to understand why things were moving so slowly. The review sheets reveal that the care team was much more concerned about Joe's behaviour and habits than came across to us in our conversations with them. We wouldn't find this out until the first professionals' meeting which was still a month away.

Joe's second weekly review

A week later Joe's second weekly review meeting brought with it the next setback. The boy who looked up from the sofa when I walked in, was a very different boy to the one I had seen on my last visit. His eyes were red, damp and puffy. He was visibly upset despite the fact he was watching a Man United match on the television.

He told me he was really down because he felt he was going backwards. After the Wednesday review meeting he had been told several things which upset him. Despite gaining over 2 kg he was told:

- he had to continue on bed-rest for the foreseeable future

- his fluid intake had to be increased as he was still showing signs of dehydration

- the doctors were considering giving him medication because they felt he was so depressedbecause he was going to the football match on Saturday with his dad, he probably wouldn't be allowed a visit home for several weeks.

I tried to calm Joe down, but I felt anger welling up inside me. We all knew that Joe's recovery phase would be difficult and for every two steps forward there would be one back. However, it seemed that Joe was being given no encouragement whatsoever. Despite the fact that he was doing everything asked of him, he seemed to be making no progress in terms of his daily routine. In addition he was putting on weight and his blood pressure and pulse were rising to more normal levels, so why was he being held back so much? Joe's reaction to today's meeting was to revert to his initial behaviour on arriving at The Great Barn. He begged and pleaded with me to take him home. He promised he would stick religiously to his re-feeding programme and he was understandably very distressed at my refusal to bow to his demands. It was also apparent that some of his previous habits were returning. He was collecting saliva in his mouth and I could see him tensing his muscles and doing his counting exercises. In turn I could feel my faith and confidence in leaving my son in this environment waning dramatically. Of course I kept this feeling from Joe.

It was time to have another meeting with Dr Cornwall. Joe really did seem to be going backwards. He had no goals to look forward to and mentally seemed to be regressing. The question of medication had reared its ugly head and both Joe and the rest of the family wanted to avoid this if at all possible. Joe didn't feel comfortable talking to any of the staff apart from Fiona. He felt that they always promised to follow things up for him but rarely seemed to do so. As a result Joe was often left feeling let down, lost and lonely. His natural reaction was to ring home and beg us to come and get him.

Time to focus

It was around this time that I decided to resign from my job. I was feeling under more and more pressure both at work and at home I felt like an elastic band being stretched to the limit. If I didn't take some of the pressure away, surely I could snap at any minute. Then I would be of no use to anyone, least of all Joe. When Joe came home I wanted to make sure I could do everything possible to help Joe avoid a relapse.

That afternoon Steve and I met with Dr Cornwall. She was hugely apologetic about the seeming collapse in communication and the fact that Joe had been so upset by feeling he was moving backwards not forwards. She explained that she felt that the lack of communication had arisen because of the absence of key members of staff over the Easter period. She also explained that because she was still quite new to the unit, there had been a period of transition while she got to know all the staff, as well as all the patients on the unit. The previous consultant had been at the unit a very long time and whilst the transition was going very well there were inevitably some hiccups.

Dr Cornwall went on to say that she was very happy with Joe's progress so far, but she had been a little concerned to see how miserable and withdrawn he had been when she had seen him on Wednesday. Now that we had explained how he felt he was moving backwards she could see why he was so upset.

We asked Dr Cornwall to fully update us of her view of the outcome of Joe's last review meeting.

First, she explained why Joe's fluid intake had to be increased. It was nothing to do with him being dehydrated. As part of his re-feeding programme his fluids had to be built up slowly to avoid re-feeding syndrome. He had started on 900 ml a day and was now being moved up to 1,500 ml a day. Eventually he would be on 1,900 ml a day so there was still some way to go.

We then talked about the issue of bed-rest. Dr Cornwall agreed with us that this seemed to be less necessary now that Joe had gained weight and his blood pressure and pulse were back to more normal levels. However, The Great Barn had its own tried and tested protocols and presumably these dictated that Joe should still be on bed-rest. She said she would discuss this with Fiona at the earliest opportunity.

Regarding medication, Dr Cornwall told us that this had been aired as a possibility later on and that Joe might benefit from taking an SSRI (type of antidepressant, for example, Prozac) to dampen down his obsessive tendencies. She assured us that we would be informed and consulted before this took place. We replied that we would rather avoid SSRIs if at all possible and Dr Cornwall agreed that it was still possible that once Joe put more weight back on his obsessive tendencies might stop by themselves.

Dr Cornwall also noted that some of the staff were slightly concerned over Joe's eating habits. It had been noted on several occasions that both Joe and the other patient on the re-feeding table had started to leave small amounts of food on their plates and hope that it wouldn't be noticed. She also said they were pushing unacceptable amounts of food off their plates, thus reducing the total amount of food they had to eat. She added that this was typical behaviour for recovering anorexics but it had to be nipped in the bud. This issue was going to be addressed at mealtimes over the next few days.

As we were having such a useful and frank discussion about Joe I decided to bring up the question of Joe's hygiene. At home Joe had been meticulous in his cleanliness, showering and washing his hair daily. However, despite the fact that Joe's review had said Joe needed to be encouraged to bath more regularly, it appeared that he hadn't washed his hair for over a week. When I had questioned Joe about this he had told me that he didn't have time to shower. He was only allowed upstairs at bedtime when he was too tired. In the morning the girls occupied all the bathrooms and in any case he didn't have time before breakfast. I had mentioned this to several members of staff but the situation hadn't improved. I told Dr Cornwall that I felt it was unacceptable to leave a 12-year-old boy to his own devices on the issue of hygiene and I felt he should be supervised. She replied that she would make sure that someone oversaw this in the future.

Looking forward to the football match

After this reassuring meeting with Dr Cornwall we went to visit Joe. He was looking forward to the football match and at least for the moment appeared to have put some of his frustrations behind him.

The member of staff on duty had put together a detailed plan for Joe's day out:

10.30 am   Snack at The Great Barn.

11.30 am   Dad to collect Joe (a packed lunch will be provided).

1.30 pm   Joe to eat packed lunch with 350 ml water.

Joe must rest for one hour after lunch.

3.45 pm   Half Time:

Joe to have snack of 150 ml milk.

Joe must rest for 30 minutes after snack.

7 pm   Joe will return to The Great Barn for supper.

Guidelines:

Joe will take minimal exercise while at the match.

There should be no discussion of food during Joe's meals/snacks.

Phone The Great Barn with any worries or concerns.

Joe was in good spirits when we left that evening. I think we all felt that a day out of The Great Barn, whilst tiring, would do Joe the world of good. It was his first major step back towards normality.

A difficult first three weeks

The first three weeks had been very difficult for everyone involved in Joe's treatment. Joe felt he was going backwards. He was doing everything asked of him but was still expected to sit around doing nothing. The days stretched endlessly in front of him. The weekends were even worse because most of his friends were allowed to go home. He had been allowed to go to the football match with his dad, but there was nothing else to look forward to. Some of the staff were OK, but there were lots of temporary staff who changed all the time. Joe didn't feel he could trust anyone.

Steve, James and I were frustrated because we felt the communication between us and the care team at The Great Barn was poor. Dr Cornwall had explained some of the reasons why, but this was not much compensation when we could see that the mixed messages were causing Joe such distress. We were delighted that Joe was gaining weight but everything seemed to be going at an excruciatingly slow pace. At times it was very tempting to simply go and get Joe and bring him home.

The care team found Joe's case difficult because there was so much intervention from the parents and in particular from me. Joe's nursing notes are full of comments suggesting that I asked too many questions and called too often. I guess this is what is often referred to as the 'overfussy mum syndrome'. I couldn't help but want to be involved. This was my son and surely I knew him best. It was inevitable that he would pour out all his questions, fears and complaints to me. When I found these to be reasonable, surely it was my duty to in turn go back to Joe's care team to clarify the issues.

Joe was successfully putting on weight, but there was still an awfully long way to go.

18. Recovering too quickly? Watch out for Rex

Joe enjoyed his football match but didn't enjoy being taken back to The Great Barn. On Sunday he once again begged me to take him home. He was convinced he was better and couldn't understand why we were still making him stay there.

Improving communication

On the Monday Steve and I had a meeting with Joe's case manager, Fiona, and his key worker, Amanda. Steve and I stated that we were both very pleased with Joe's progress, but that we still felt that there were problems with communication between the family and the care team. It was particularly important to resolve this issue as Steve was going back to New Zealand in a few days' time. Fiona agreed to have a regular meeting with me, which would be arranged in advance. She would also give me her shift schedule so that I could fax it to Steve. This would enable Steve to contact Fiona for regular updates. I also agreed to fax Steve a copy of the decisions from the weekly review meeting. In future I agreed to try not to get into lengthy discussions with other members of staff unless it was unavoidable, e.g. if both Fiona and Amanda were sick.

Joe's third weekly review

This review represented a major step forward for several reasons. Joe's blood pressure and pulse had settled into a more normal range and his weight had increased to 36 kg from 35.3 kg. Joe had started joining in with some of the activities at the day centre and was due to start art therapy the following week. However, the big news that Joe had been waiting for was that he no longer had to lie down on his bed for his rest periods. His rest periods would still be of the same length, but he would be allowed to sit in the lounge watching TV with the other patients. This was a major step forward for Joe and immediately made him feel like a more normal person. In addition the care team had agreed that Joe could have a few hours out at the weekend with his family. There was still a long way to go, but at least Joe could see he was making some positive progress.

Returning to normality?

For a child who has been totally cocooned in an institution for a month, trips out are a major event. Joe had coped very well with his trip to the football match, which was a good sign, but we still had to be careful not to try and move things on too quickly. The care team advised us that a trip to the local cinema was often a good idea in these early stages. We took Joe to see Ice Age, which both Joe and Tom enjoyed. It was the first time for months that I had seen the two boys so relaxed together. When we got back to The Great Barn we sat in the garden chatting for a while before it was time for Joe to go in for tea. It had been a successful outing.

On Sunday it was a beautiful day. I visited Joe in the morning and we spent some time in the garden. Joe seemed brighter in mood. He said he had enjoyed his trip out but that he found it very difficult returning to The Great Barn. He explained that he found the weekends much more difficult than the weekdays because most of the other residents went home on Friday afternoon and didn't return until Sunday evening. In addition the staff on duty at weekends were often temporary staff who Joe didn't really feel he could relate to. I sympathised with his frustrations, but tried to reassure him over how much progress he had made already. If he carried on being fully compliant perhaps he would be allowed to come home in a few weekends time.

We then spent twenty minutes playing catch with a tennis ball and then a rugby ball. We had done this a couple of times before. Joe knew he wasn't allowed to run around, but enjoyed being able to do something vaguely sporty in the fresh air. I became aware that one of the staff was keeping a close eye on us through the window. I then made a very poor throw that Joe had no chance of catching. He skipped across the grass to retrieve the ball and immediately the window was thrown open and we were told in no uncertain terms that it was time to come in. We returned to the lounge and spent the remainder of my visit watching TV. Joe was quiet but didn't comment on this latest episode. He was learning that things were going to move forward at a slow pace and that we all simply had to accept that fact. I was to find out later that several of the care staff felt that Joe was being far too active in the garden and that they clearly felt I should have been stopping him.

Art therapy

On Monday Joe started art therapy. Thus far Joe had found his trips to the day centre pretty boring. He was still deemed too sick to join in with lessons and so had spent most of his time there sitting around or playing pool. Art therapy was a welcome break and because Joe thought there would be no pressure to discuss his feelings and/or problems, he approached it in a positive mood. However, in the session Joe did have to describe his feelings at one point and became tearful and upset. He said his main problem was that he was bored, but when encouraged to explore this further, he did acknowledge that he was experiencing lots of other feelings, both happy and sad. When I visited that evening I asked Joe about his first session. He said that for the most part he had enjoyed it. He was given the option to paint a picture or make a clay model. He had made a model of a footballer which he was clearly very pleased with, but he was a little bemused when the art teacher had sat down with him at the end of the lesson to discuss his work. She asked Joe why he had made this footballer. He replied that he loved football and couldn't wait to start playing again. She agreed that it was good for Joe to have things to look forward to, but suggested that he must be feeling lonely because he had only made one footballer. Joe felt that she was reading too much into things, but the most important thing was that he had enjoyed the session and was looking forward to the next one. The session had certainly prompted Joe to address his feelings, which was a good thing. I asked Joe what other therapy he was having. He told me that he had started joining in with the group therapy sessions and that he found it quite easy to express his feelings in front of his peers. In contrast he was not enjoying his sessions with Fiona his key worker. He had never found it easy to converse with adults on a one-to-one basis and this was proving to be no exception. Fiona wasn't pushing him in these sessions but was gently trying to probe into his mind to find out what was upsetting him. Joe found these sessions distressing because he couldn't find the right words to express his feelings. His response was to keep saying over and over that he didn't think he had a problem anymore and would like to go home as soon as possible.

Two steps forward, one step back, is Rex still there?

Whereas the previous week had been very positive, with all of us feeling that Joe was making excellent progress, the next week was going to be much more difficult. Several members of staff made it clear that they felt Joe was being moved forward too quickly and when Joe picked up on this he became very angry and frustrated again. Was his anger an indication that he was still very much being controlled by Rex and that he wanted to get home as quickly as possible so that Rex could take over again? Or did Joe genuinely want to get better and put Rex behind him? At this stage nobody knew the answer to these questions.

Joe's fourth weekly review

The key feature of this review was the question of whether Joe was being too active at this relative early stage. Joe's weight was still increasing but the rate of increase had slowed down, as Joe had become more active. His weight was now 36.7 kg, an increase of 0.7 kg over the week before. The care team had specifically requested clear guidance from Joe's medical team on the issue of activity levels, as they felt that both Joe and I were pushing the boundaries.

Joe's therapeutic programme was gradually being built up. This week Joe's care team decided it was time to book a family therapy consultation and to consider cognitive behavioural therapy. Joe's care team were still concerned about Joe's ritualistic behaviour. Joe claimed he carried on with his rituals because he was so bored and frustrated with the lack of physical activity. He also claimed that he was unable to sleep properly because of this.

Frustrations abound

After the huge progress of the previous week, Joe was not impressed with the outcome of this week's review meeting. Bed-rest was now a dim and distant memory and Joe was desperate to be able to be more active. However, every time he skipped across the room or ran to pick up a ball that was being played with outside, he was severely reprimanded. On the Wednesday and Friday evenings when I visited Joe was extremely distressed. I tried to talk reason with him in his room but he started screaming, shouting and hitting his head against the wall. On both occasions once he had calmed down he was very subdued and tearful. I could understand why Joe was so frustrated with the slow progress, but I could also understand why his care team wanted to take things slowly. I tried to sympathise with Joe without making any rash promises about when he would be able to be more active. I had to accept that Joe's frustration and anger was part and parcel of an anorexic's long road to recovery.

Another issue for Joe was that he desperately wanted to come home at the weekends. It had been decided at the review meeting that Joe could have just two hours out again at the weekend. Going to the cinema seemed the easiest thing to do and Joe asked if he could invite a friend along. This was a positive sign. He still wanted to keep in contact with his friends from school. It is often the case that recovering anorexics choose to hide away from the outside world for as long as possible. On Saturday we went to see Bend It Like Beckham. Joe dutifully had his snack of milk at the normal time and even asked for some sweets, although not surprisingly he only ate a couple of them. Whilst he was clearly pleased to have escaped the confines of The Great Barn I could see he was still feeling ill at ease and much of the time during the film he sat forward and tensed his muscles. He was very quiet when we left the cinema and ignored his friend's attempts to engage in conversation. I could feel trouble was brewing. Sure enough, when we got to the car Joe burst into tears and refused to get in. He pleaded with me to take him home. Couldn't I see how much better he was? He promised he would eat enough to carry on gaining weight but he couldn't bear going back to The Great Barn. Once again I was emotionally torn in two. I desperately wanted to take him home but I knew how dangerous that would be. Eventually I persuaded Joe to get back in the car and we returned to the Great Barn. Joe seemed to manage to pull himself together and chatted with his friend in the lounge while I reported back to the care worker on duty. She wasn't at all surprised that Joe had been tense and upset. Joe was making fantastic progress but there was still an awfully long way to go. I was feeling very tearful by this stage and the care worker asked me if I ever let Joe see how upset I was. I said I tried to be strong in front of him, otherwise I feared he might try and manipulate me into letting him come home. She fully understood this but suggested that this was an issue that could be explored in family therapy. Our family therapy sessions were due to start in a couple of weeks. She also suggested that we could discuss this issue at the next carers support group as it was common for parents' of children at The Great Barn to feel pressurised and manipulated by their children.

Chest pains – another step back?

On Sunday morning Joe complained to the staff on duty that he was feeling chest pains. He felt his heart was trying to beat too fast and he felt uncomfortable. When checked, his pulse, blood pressure and temperature wcre in the normal range and so the care team did some relaxation exercises with Joe. The duty doctor was informed and he advised the care team to monitor Joe carefully over the next few hours.

James, Tom and I arrived mid-morning and we were informed that Joe was being closely monitored. Joe was extremely subdued and after an hour asked us to leave because he wanted to be on his own and he found our presence upsetting.

Joe was low in mood all afternoon and had to be persuaded to join in with games with the other patients. After dinner he complained of chest pains again and became very frightened, thinking he was having a heart attack. Once again the care team reassured Joe, took him through some relaxation exercises and explained that anxiety can cause pains like these to happen. Once Joe had calmed down one of the care team phoned me to let me know of this latest episode. We agreed that it was probably best if I didn't speak to Joe that evening because he was using me as an outlet for his anger and frustration. It was better to let him cool off and I could see him again the next day.

Half an hour later Joe was on the phone to me. He had waited for his rest period to finish and then at the earliest opportunity had rushed to the phone. Once again he begged me to take him home. He said he didn't trust any of the staff and he hadn't seen his key worker Fiona for days, so he might as well come home. Once again I had to put my hard-hearted hat on and gently explain all the reasons why he needed to stay at The Great Barn. Joe was very angry and accused me of giving up on him and not caring about him. As always I told him I loved him very much but that I couldn't bring him home until he was much better. It was an awful conversation and Joe was still sobbing when I put the phone down.

I called the staff phone half an hour later and was reassured to hear that Joe was in a better mood. I reiterated how important I felt it was for Joe to have as much contact as possible with his key worker, Fiona, as he felt it difficult talking to other members of staff. I was assured that she would spend some time with Joe the next day.

Getting better but feeling worse

I had a long conversation with Fiona the next day. Joe had had a fitful night and the staff on duty had observed that he had slept in a tightly curled foetal position. Fiona spent several hours with Joe after breakfast and for once he had engaged in conversation. He had explained that he was feeling very homesick over the weekend and had taken things out on his mum by shouting at her and saying some things he didn't mean. He said the chest pains had frightened him but accepted that these were caused by his anxiety. He felt that the relaxation exercises had helped and he would be happy to do them again. Fiona had discussed with Joe several ways of coping with stress and written them down for him:

- Be aware of emotions causing distress.

- Use a diary if necessary to help identify and make sense of these emotions.

- Discuss feelings with others if you feel able to.

- If conflicts with others arise, try to resolve these by speaking directly to the person concerned or by writing a letter, or trying to communicate in some other way.

- Practise relaxation techniques with staff. These guidelines all made sense to me, and Fiona seemed to think Joe had taken them on board. She went on to explain the key points that she would be discussing with Joe's consultant psychiatrist following the events of the weekend:

- Further work was needed with Joe regarding relaxation techniques and anxiety management.

- Joe's physical observations would continue to be measured on a weekly basis, but it was now more important for staff to assess Joe's mood.

- Now that Joe was physically stronger Fiona would be exploring Joe's emotional and psychological feeling about his anorexia. This process would inevitably lead to an increase in Joe's anxiety levels.

- This process could also result in an increase in Joe's compulsive behaviour and obsessional thoughts. Fiona would be monitoring these very carefully.

- Now that Joe's physical observations were within the normal range Fiona felt it would be appropriate for him to be allowed a little exercise time twice a day. She suggested that this would start off at 15 minutes per half day and would be increased gradually as long as Joe continued to be compliant and gain weight.

- Repeat blood tests and further medical investigations might be required as Joe gained further weight and became more active.

A little activity goes a long way

Sure enough later that day Joe was told that he was going to be allowed 15 minutes exercise per shift (half day). There were strict guidelines accompanying this new privilege. Joe must inform staff of his intended activity, which might be playing in the garden with the other patients, playing football in the yard etc. Joe could choose to walk to and from the day centre rather than being driven, but this would count as part of his activity. If Joe abused his new privilege or was non-compliant then his next exercise session would be cancelled.

Joe was ecstatic at hearing of his newly found freedom, but immediately overstepped the mark. After 15 minutes of playing hide and seek in the garden with the other patients, one of the staff on duty called him in. Joe immediately climbed a tree and then, from the tree, tried to argue that he was owed another 15 minutes because he hadn't had any exercise that morning. He became extremely angry and aggressive when this was refused and as a result he lost the next morning's exercise privilege. A hard lesson for Joe to learn, but the rules had been very clearly explained to him.

Our second parents/carers' meeting

Tom came with me to visit Joe that evening. I knew that both Joe and Tom felt awkward with each other at the moment, but I felt it was important to maintain some sort of contact. I left them watching TV together so that I could attend the parent/carers meeting. As before, I naturally ended up talking to the parents of the other anorexic parents. It turned out that Emma was now making much better progress. Her weight had been stable for two months, her visits home had been much less traumatic and she had slowly been reintegrated back into her normal school. Her parents were hopeful for a discharge within the next month, which would mean her stay at The Great Barn had been nine months. I was heartened to hear of this progress, but hoped Joe would not have to stay for such a long time.

The other two girls had still not reached their target weight and their parents fully expected their daughters to be at The Great Barn for some time to come. We talked about several things during the course of the meeting, but the two issues I found most useful that we discussed were the anger and aggression of anorexia, and family therapy.

Angry Anna and Raging Rex

One of the most difficult things for the carers of an anorexic child to cope with is the unpredictable mood swings and aggressive behaviour. In the meeting I discovered that we all felt that our child's mind had been taken over by some sort of monster. As I explained earlier in this book I referred to this monster as Rex, many carers of girls refer to the female version of this monster as Anna.

I described how Joe had been screaming and shouting at me, telling me I didn't care about him. Sometimes he would hit his head against the wall.

The other parents nodded knowingly.

I described how Joe begged and pleaded with me to bring him home. If I didn't he would commit suicide.

The other parents nodded knowingly.

I described how Joe ranted and raved about how none of the staff listened to him, they didn't understand him and he didn't trust them.

The other parents nodded knowingly.

We talked about coping strategies. We all felt that the most important thing was to keep calm and to be consistent in terms of response. There was absolutely no point in making promises you couldn't keep. There was no point being angry or shouting back. Sometimes it was worth pointing out how hurtful or unreasonable the child was being and very often this led to some sort of apology later on. We all agreed it was very important to let the child know that you loved them very much, but that you didn't like the effect anorexia was having on them. We all agreed that however much you knew your child was going to be unreasonable and aggressive, it didn't make it any easier to cope with. Sessions such as these parent/carer meetings are very useful, but it is also very important to give yourself 'time out' after a visit from angry Anna or raging Rex. We all had different ways of relaxing and letting off steam and we all agreed that it was crucial to indulge yourself every so often.

Family therapy

Most professional experts in the field of eating disorders in young people will agree that family therapy is one of the most important ways of combating the disease. Our first family therapy session had been booked for a couple of weeks' time. Two of the families represented in this parents/carers' meeting had undergone several sessions and so I was intrigued to hear their views. Both families had found the first session very awkward, they didn't know what was expected of them and naturally felt a little defensive. One of the Dads said he came out of the first session and realised he had spent the whole session apologising to his daughter for a whole range of things that were part of his everyday life. These included leaving early for work, going on business trips, watching sport on TV and occasionally playing golf at the weekend. Having thought about it afterwards he realised that his daughter was crying out for more attention from him. Both families agreed that family therapy was a good forum for the whole family to air their thoughts or concerns. Nobody really looked forward to these sessions but at the very worst no harm was done, and at the very best problems that had previously gone unnoticed could be resolved. All in all it was a very useful parents/carers' meeting.

By the time I came out of the meeting Joe was at the re-feeding table having his snack. Tom was still watching TV. Joe was tearful and seemed subdued but couldn't really explain why. It had been an emotional weekend and the chest pains had scared him. He wanted to get better as quickly as possible and to come home and be normal. I guessed that the chest pains had made him realise that he was still pretty fragile and there was still a long way to go to full recovery. I gave Joe a long reassuring hug and then took Tom home.

Cognitive behavioural therapy

At our next regular meeting with Fiona, Steve and I had a long discussion with her about Joe's progress. Fiona explained that she couldn't force Joe to discuss his difficulties with her. She also said that it was not unusual for young children to take a long time to build up trust and to engage with their key worker. I wondered if there were any other options to try and get Joe to talk about his problems and we all agreed that it was worth trying cognitive behavioural therapy (CBT). Fiona arranged for Steve and I to meet with George, the CB therapist at the day centre. We immediately took to him. He was young and enthusiastic and explained things in a very clear manner. He told us that he would offer Joe a session later that week. The first few sessions would be very low key and the aim would be to build a relationship and get to know each other. If these were successful George would start challenging Joe's beliefs, anxieties and any negative thoughts. Joe would be asked to keep a diary of such thoughts and hopefully in time would be able to start identifying why many of these thoughts were illogical and/or irrational. George explained that most of his patients were older than Joe and he thought that Joe might still be a little young for CBT, but it was certainly worth a try.

Joe's fifth weekly review

Joe's weight had increased to 37.2 kg from 36.7 kg. The dietician had set Joe's target weight at 38 to 40 kg so he was not far off. However it was evident that Joe's care team were still worried about Joe's ritualistic behaviour and some of the staff suspected that Joe was exercising in secret. His weight gain of just 0.5 kg supported the view that he was doing too much too quickly. The care team were also concerned that Joe continued to air his anxieties with me, stating that he could not speak to the staff about things that were worrying him. They also noted that Joe was displaying manipulative tendencies and continued to spend a great deal of time trying to persuade me to take him home.

Joe's hygiene had continued to leave a lot to be desired, with Joe stating he did not have time to bath, so it was agreed that I would supervise Joe having a shower on a Friday evening.

Despite these concerns it was recognised that Joe needed to feel he was making some progress. It was agreed that Joe could come home for all three days of the Bank holiday weekend as long as he returned to The Great Barn for his meals. In addition his exercise guidelines were to be increased to 20 minutes per shift.

Allowed home at the weekend

We were all delighted at the prospect of Joe coming home for the bank holiday weekend. As always there were strict guidelines and Joe had to return to The Great Barn for his meals. Thankfully he was allowed his mid-morning and mid-afternoon snack at home or we would have spent the whole weekend in the car. Added to the excitement of coming home, Joe was pleased to hear that he was now allowed 20 minutes exercise per shift. Whilst he would have liked even more freedom he could see that he was making clear progress.

I picked Joe up at 9.30 on Saturday morning. He had just finished his hour rest after breakfast and was keen to leave as quickly as possible. I was reminded to give Joe his snack (glass of milk) at 11 am and that I should supervise his half an hour rest period after this. I should avoid letting Joe spend long periods in his bedroom on his own and keep an eye on how long his visits to the toilet were. Joe had to be back at The Great Barn by 12.30 pm for lunch.

Joe had asked me to arrange a hair cut and so we picked up his brother Tom and went straight to the hairdresser. Joe had his hair cut first whilst I chatted with Tom. Then the plan was that Joe would wait with me whilst Tom had his hair cut. Joe had other ideas. He felt I should let him walk home on his own. After all it was all down hill and only five minutes away. This wasn't an unreasonable request but I didn't think I should let him go. What if he ran all the way and had a heart attack? There were a few uneasy moments when I thought Joe was going to create a major scene, but after whispering to me that I didn't care about him, didn't trust him and was ruining his life, Joe calmed down and waited patiently for Tom's haircut to be finished.

By the time we got home it was time for Joe's snack, after which we played cards for half an hour. Then we all played a game of catching the tennis ball in the garden. Before we knew it, it was time to take Joe back to The Great Barn for lunch. I dropped him off at 12.30 pm and then went shopping in the local town. I returned to The Great Barn at 2 pm to find Joe happily chatting with a member of staff about his morning's activities.

That afternoon I had arranged for a couple of Joe's friends to come round. It was lovely to see them playing in the garden. Joe was laughing and seemed totally relaxed. I called them all in for a drink at 3.30 pm and so Joe was able to have his snack without it seeming to be a chore. Then the three boys sat and watched sport on TV for the rest of the afternoon. Joe seemed so normal. There was no sign of his compulsive exercising or other obsessional tendencies. For the first time in months I felt myself relax and I could start looking forward to the time when our family would return to normal. Joe chatted happily all the way back to The Great Barn and gave me a big hug before going in for his dinner.

Sunday and Monday followed a similar pattern. We played some games as a family, Joe had some friends round and I took him to visit a couple of friends.

Inevitably he was more active than if he had spent the weekend at The Great Barn, but he was very compliant each time I called him in for a snack or to do a less energetic activity. Apart from the episode in the hairdresser there was no sign of tension or depression all weekend. I was a little disappointed that Joe and Tom didn't do more together, but I could see that Tom was still a bit nervous about his older brother's state of mind. The one activity they did do together was to spend about fifteen minutes bouncing on the trampoline.

141

Tom wanted to show Joe some of his new tricks and I reasoned that as long as Joe didn't over do it, it was positive that the two boys were doing something together.

Vulnerable to losing weight

Joe was a little subdued when I drove him back to The Great Barn on Monday evening. We had all had such a lovely weekend and he clearly wasn't looking forward to being back under the strict supervision of the staff at The Great Barn. As soon as we arrived one of the members of staff on duty took me aside to ask for feedback of our weekend. I gave her a brief outline of events and admitted that Joe had probably been a little more active than he should have been, playing football and cricket with his friends and bouncing on the trampoline for a short period with his brother. This didn't go down too well and I was given quite a lecture about how Joe should only be doing a very limited amount of gentle activity and that he was still very vulnerable to losing weight. There seemed little point in arguing, so I simply agreed that we would be very careful in future. However, deep down I felt that Joe had had an excellent weekend and become much stronger mentally. He had coped extremely well being back in his home environment and had no problems integrating with his friends. His activity levels had been way below what they would normally be in his home environment, albeit a little more than he was allowed within the confines of The Great Barn. He had been in very good spirits all weekend and had not displayed any obsessional tendencies. I prayed that he had not lost weight. We would soon find out.

Cognitive behavioural therapy

Joe had his first cognitive behavioural therapy session with George. George explained to Joe what CBT is and that the first few sessions would be very relaxed with the aim of getting to know each other. Joe was reluctant to talk very much at first and George felt he was very shy and anxious. However, by the end of the session Joe had clearly decided he liked George and had started to tell George about his sporting achievements at school. They arranged to meet at the same time the following week.

Art therapy

Joe had his second art therapy session. In this session he chose to make two clay figures. This time they were skateboarders. The art therapist suggested that Joe must be feeling less lonely because he had made two figures this time, but perhaps he was still feeling vulnerable because it is easy for skateboarders to fall over. Joe thought this was quite a good point but he still found it difficult to discuss his feelings and became tearful in the discussion session. Clearly art therapy was having a positive effect as it was helping Joe to address his feelings. He was still finding it difficult to do this in his one-to-one sessions with Fiona. Joe continued with art therapy for six weeks. As the weeks progressed he participated more in the group discussions and used several different art materials to express his feelings. He was able to distinguish between the anorexic Joe who did too much exercise and didn't eat enough, and a healthier Joe as he used to be and, hopefully, as he would be in the future.

Joe's sixth weekly review

Joe continued to gain weight despite his increased activity levels at the weekend. His weight increased to 37.8 kg from 37.2 kg. He continued to be in good spirits, was fully compliant with re-feeding programme and attended the day centre without any problems.

Despite continued concerns over Joe's ritualistic tendencies and suspicions that he was exercising in secret, it was decided that Joe could have his first meal at home at the weekend. It was also recognised that it was inevitable that Joe would be more active at home than he was within the confines of The Great Barn. During the week Joe's exercise guidelines were increased to half an hour per shift. If Joe was more active than this at the weekend then we should increase his calorie intake accordingly.

Lunch at home

Another week and another big step forward. The fact that Joe was going to be allowed to have lunch at home meant we could have a much more relaxing weekend with much less time in the car going to and from The Great Barn. I have to admit that we were all slightly nervous. All Joe's meals thus far had been at the re-feeding table under close supervision from a member of staff. How would Joe cope with sitting at the family dining table for his lunch on both days? Would he be fully compliant, would he try to negotiate smaller portions or would he refuse to eat altogether? We had heard several horror stories about the first meals at home.

We were given specific guidelines for that weekend, which made our life a lot easier. If Joe decided to become non-compliant simply because he was at home then we could refer him to the guidelines. The guidelines were as follows:

- **Home visit**. Joe is to be collected at 9.30 am and returned to the unit by 5.30 pm.

- **Supervision**. Joe is nursed at The Great Barn on level two observations (officially checking his whereabouts every 30 minutes), but generally staff know his whereabouts at all times. For meals and rest periods Joe should be under constant supervision and he is not allowed to go to the toilet during these times. When Joe does go to the toilet an 'appropriate' amount of time should be given prior to checking. If Joe is subtly exercising on rests or 'in secret' he should be confronted and told to stop. Furthermore his exercise should be stopped for the day. It is also suggested that any unusual behaviour, for example, superstitious or ritualistic should be confronted and support should be given to Joe to help him stop.

- **Exercise**. Joe is allowed 30 minutes exercise in the morning and 30 minutes in the afternoon – this is gentle exercise, not aerobic. Joe is expected to walk rather than run between exercise and not to be 'on the go' all day.

- **Meals**. Joe's snacks consist of 150 ml of milk at 10.45 am and 3.30 pm.
  Lunch for Saturday is cheeseburger, chips and salad followed by a choc-ice, and accompanied by 350 ml of a soft drink.
  Lunch for Sunday is cheese omelette with French bread followed by fresh fruit, ice cream and chocolate sauce.
  We were given specific measurements of all the ingredients for both meals.

We had a fairly quiet Saturday morning and Joe happily had his snack and rest mid-morning. Both Joe and Tom were happy to have burger and chips for lunch followed by a choc-ice. They both cleared their plates and there were no complaints. In the afternoon we went to the boys school to watch a cricket match in which several of Joe's friends were playing. It was a five-minute walk from home and Joe was very quiet. As we approached the school gates Joe admitted that he was feeling very nervous, but he still wanted to go in. Fortunately Joe's team were batting and within minutes Joe was happily sat in their midst enjoying watching the opening batsmen hitting the ball all around the pitch. We stayed for an hour then walked home for Joe's snack. He had clearly enjoyed being back in his old school environment, albeit briefly, but was tired from the experience. He was contented to sit and watch sport on the TV for the rest of the afternoon until it was time to take him back to The Great Barn.

On Sunday I picked Joe up at 9.30 am as arranged. We visited one of his friends on the way home and he had his snack and rest without any fuss. The two boys played on the Playstation in Joe's rest period and then played in the garden for half an hour before we returned home for lunch.

Lunch was a little more difficult than the previous day. James had taken Tom and his three children out for the day so it was just Joe and me at home for lunch. When I announced that we were going to have a cheese omelette Joe freaked out. He said he had never eaten a cheese omelette in his life and he wasn't going to start now. I had visions of having to drag Joe kicking and screaming back to The Great Barn and I wanted to avoid this at all costs. One of the problems was that at The Great Barn the patients were allowed to have three food exemptions. Joe had chosen cheesecake, tomatoes and eggs on their own. He assumed that this would include omelette, which he would never have had at home even before his anorexia took hold. I could see his point and agreed to ring The Great Barn to see what we should do. The nurse on duty was very sympathetic and said there had clearly been a mistake. Luckily she had access to other meal plans with the same calorific value and we settled on jacket potato with cheese and beans. The crisis was averted and Joe happily ate every morsel.

That afternoon some friends came round and played on the Playstation with Joe for a couple of hours, which covered his snack and rest period. They played football in the garden for half an hour before I took him back. It had been lovely seeing Joe so happy all weekend. There had been no evidence of secret exercising or ritualistic behaviour and apart from the near crisis over the omelette Joe had been very relaxed all weekend. Joe was a little tearful on the way back, but didn't try to persuade me to take him back home.

Cognitive behavioural therapy

Joe had his second cognitive behavioural session with George. Having established a reasonable level of trust in the first session Joe was more talkative in this session and was able to talk openly about events leading up to his illness and the period in which he lost weight. George quickly established that Joe had perfectionist tendencies and could not cope with failure. Joe's self-esteem had fallen during his illness and he very much believed that his peers were better than he was both academically and on the sports field. Over the course of the next six weeks George continued to work with Joe, helping him to identify and then challenge some of these negative thoughts. In addition George attempted to examine Joe's ritualistic and obsessive tendencies that the care team felt were still in evidence in Joe's behaviour at The Great Barn. It was difficult for George to make much progress in this area however as Joe was adamant that he had stopped all these habits since he had put on weight. Joe recognised that he had been obsessed about exercise, that he had developed superstitious behaviour and that he had developed many other rituals, but that he had stopped all these things within a few weeks of being at The Great Barn.

Joe's seventh weekly review

Joe's weight had increased to 38.9 kg from 37.8 kg , so he was well within his target weight of 38 kg to 40 kg . In eight weeks Joe had gained just under 8 kg , which was a fantastic achievement. Joe desperately wanted to leave The Great Barn and come home, but there was still a long way to go. The care team were still concerned about his ritualistic tendencies. Staff still suspected Joe was exercising in secret and Joe had been observed doing discreet exercises during the community meeting and hopping and skipping on the walk to the day centre. It had also been noted that Joe was becoming much more assertive and that he had requested shorter rest periods. It was clear that the care team felt that Joe was fighting against them rather than working with them.

Despite these concerns it was agreed that Joe's rest periods should be halved and that he could spend the weekend, including Saturday night at home.

Family therapy

James, Joe, Tom and I attended our first family therapy session at the day centre. Tom was just nine years old and was very nervous at the prospect of having to talk to a stranger. He spent most of the session sitting on the floor drawing pictures. Joe was in a defiant mood and didn't see why he should have to endure yet another type of therapy. He had had enough of The Great Barn and wanted to go home. Within minutes of the session starting he had told the therapist that there was nothing wrong with his home life, the only problem he had was having to stay at The Great Barn. Joe clearly felt he had said his piece and refused to say another word for the rest of the session.

James and I spent the rest of the time filling the therapist in on our family background. She agreed that it was a fairly complex set-up, but not particularly unusual these days. She also reassured us that anorexia could strike any type of family, from the simplest nuclear family to the most complex extended family, and from the most underprivileged classes to the most privileged classes.

We talked through some of the changes that had occurred in the family set-up in the last few years and how the boys had coped with such things as their father living abroad, James moving in, moving school and moving house. It was really a getting to know each other session although the boys were so quiet that we almost forgot they were there. A second session was scheduled for the following week.

The first night at home

As for the previous weekend we were given detailed instructions by the care team.

- **Home visit**. Joe is to be collected after breakfast on Saturday and returned Sunday in time for tea.

- **Supervision**. We were advised to refer back to the supervision notes for the previous week and the following additional advice was given. Joe acts out superstitious behaviour or engages in (secret) exercise when stressed or upset. Be vigilant that Joe is not exercising when alone in the bedroom. Offer support by encouraging him to talk about his thoughts and feelings and anything that might have upset him that day. If his behaviour is inappropriate encourage him to stop and offer support.

- **Meals**. Joe's menu for the weekend was as follows:
  Saturday lunch was BBQ pork chops followed by Angel Delight.
  Saturday tea was jacket potato with baked beans and cheese followed by a low fat yoghurt.
  Sunday breakfast was a bowl of cereal with semi-skimmed milk and two pieces of toast, butter and jam.
  Sunday lunch was two rounds of tuna mayonnaise sandwich followed by fruit salad with double cream.
  We were given specific measurements of all the ingredients for both meals as well as guidance for Joe's fluid intake.

How to make a normal meal into a re-feeding meal

In contrast to the meal guidance for the previous week, the menus we were given gave instructions for a normal portion and then what needed to be added to make it into a re-feeding meal. For example, I had to add two teaspoons of butter to Joe's mashed potato; add two tablespoons of double cream to his Angel Delight and add an extra tablespoon of mayonnaise to his tuna sandwiches. This helped me enormously when Joe was discharged from The Great Barn and we no longer had the security of detailed meal plans. I was well prepared in the art of adjusting Joe's calorie intake to reflect his activity levels and to gain additional weight when his target weight range was increased.

Despite having to eat more than everyone else Joe coped admirably at the meal table. The only time he tried to resist the allocated amount of food was on the Sunday morning when he asked if he could have just one piece of toast. When I explained he would have to go back to The Great Barn early if he didn't eat all his food he reluctantly agreed to have two pieces.

Joe appeared very relaxed all weekend. We went to the cinema on Saturday afternoon and he had some friends around on Sunday. He slept peacefully and there was no evidence of ritualistic or obsessive behaviour, or secret exercising.

Joe's eighth weekly review

Joe's normal review meeting was replaced this week by his first professionals' meeting. This was a major event and Joe, James and I were all very nervous about it. It took the same format as the weekly multidisciplinary review meeting. The key difference was that outside professionals and parents were invited. This included Joe's form teacher Mr Dunston and Dr Davis, the child psychiatrist from our local Child & Family Mental Health Unit. Our GP was also invited but sent his apologies. This was the first opportunity for us to establish exactly how much progress Joe's care team really thought he had made. Thus far the feedback from each weekly meeting had simply been to tell us Joe's weight and the decisions for the coming week. We were unaware for example that Joe's obsessive and ritualistic tendencies were still so much in evidence on the unit.

Several of the other parents that we had met at the parents/carers meetings had warned us that the first professionals' meeting could be difficult. Comments by staff about the parents or the home environment could be upsetting.

The night before the professionals' meeting I had a very distressed phone call from Joe. He had been talking to Fiona and had mentioned that he wanted to start school reintegration before the end of term. Fiona had not even thought about school reintegration yet and so had been non-committal to Joe. Joe had interpreted this as a sign that he would be kept at The Great Barn throughout the summer holidays. Because I couldn't make him any promises he slammed the phone down on me.

I rang and asked the nurse on duty to check that Joe was OK. He had gone to his bedroom and she found him in floods of tears. He told the nurse that he had been told he would be at The Great Barn for about three months and now he was being told he would be there until September. He hated The Great Barn and he hated all the staff. They were all liars and kept moving the goal posts. The nurse tried to calm him down by telling him that whatever is best for him would be decided by everyone, including his mum, at the professionals' meeting the next day. Apparently he calmed down but had a restless night.

Professionals' meeting

Everyone sat round in a big circle. Fiona had put together a report on Joe, which was similar to the weekly review sheets but with more detailed comments and explanation. A summary of her report follows.

Professionals' report

1. Physical

- After initial resistance Joe has been fully compliant with his re-feeding programme. Joe now weighs 39.3 kg. His target weight is 38 kg to 40 kg.

- On admission Joe's blood pressure and pulse were bradycardic. He had been admitted to his local hospital as an emergency three days previously with concerns that he may have been having a cardiac arrest. Since then his physical observations have settled within normal limits. He complained of chest pains on 24th April, but these appear to have been anxiety induced.

- Joe is currently allowed half an hour exercise per shift. However, staff suspect Joe is secretly exercising. This was more apparent on admission, but staff have also reported recently that Joe displays ritualistic behaviour relating to exercise in certain situations such as the community meeting and on his rest periods.

- Joe wakes early and his sleep is somewhat disruptive. More recently Joe has been going to the toilet more often in the night. Staff suspect he may be exercising and/or vomiting. A period of level four observation should be considered to assess this better.

2. Hygiene

- Joe changes his clothes regularly and always looks well groomed.

- Joe did not want to bath at The Great Barn saying he did not have time. This is an objectively irrational explanation. Joe's mum now oversees his weekly bathing. Joe's hygiene standards seem to have improved and he now says he would like to shower without prompting.

3. Social interactions

- Initially Joe was aloof from others and was quiet and tearful at times.

- Now Joe is accepted as part of the group. He is polite, chatty, witty and has a good sense of humour with staff and peers alike on the unit.

- Joe has managed to keep up with school friends and has attended a concert at main stream school, which he was a little anxious about but enjoyed. Joe sees school friends on his leave home every weekend.

4. Cognitive

- Joe wants to get better and be discharged as soon as possible.

- Joe has become very frustrated, angry and upset with his mum if the plan is not moving as quickly as he wishes.

- Joe suggests that his limited activity is making him bored and that each week he needs to see a change in his care plan to know he ismaking progress.

- Joe has had three sessions of cognitive behavioural therapy. His therapist has reported that it has been difficult to socialise Joe into the CBT model. Joe is clearly demonstrating obsessive patterns and the next session will focus on attempting to examine this.

- Joe has found it difficult to engage with his case manager and the relationship is still in the early stages of building trust and rapport. Joe avoids telling his case manager his true thoughts and feelings. However, Joe has more recently been able to identify that he exercises and acts out compulsions when he is upset. As a result of this breakthrough, Joe and his case manager agreed that it would be helpful to Joe if staff were to discreetly stop him acting out ritualistic behaviour giving him support to discuss what's on his mind. In addition, if Joe is caught exercising in secret, his planned activities or exercise will be stopped for that day.

- Joe eats very quickly and sometimes appears to struggle with his fluids. He was very angry when challenged over this, but has managed to slow down. Staff still notice some ritualistic behaviour at mealtimes such as moving cutlery and praying under his breath.

- Other than exercising Joe is age appropriate and compliant with the unit's limits and boundaries.

5. Family

- Joe lives with his mother, stepfather and younger brother.

- His father lives in New Zealand, but visited the UK for a month when Joe was first ill to give support. Joe's father is kept updated by Joe's mother and he phones regularly.

- Family therapy has started; incorporating the family members Joe resides with.

- Joe has mentioned that he dislikes being the eldest sibling, as he feels he always gets the blame when things go wrong. Otherwise he seems to get on well with all family members, although at times he doesn't get on with his younger brother.

- Joe's mother and stepfather visit regularly and are very involved with his plan of care. Mother has been very anxious at times and has needed constant reassurance from the nursing and multidisciplinary team. This anxiety is understandable as anorexia is a life threatening illness and parents were no doubt worried about Joe's health and prognosis prior to and during admission. However, on occasions the team has met with family together in order to try and keep the care plan united. Mother is keen to advocate for her son and uses her insight of Joe to advise staff of his needs. At times the nursing staff have felt that the rate at which such requests are made are a little too fast for comfort.

- Essentially though, Joe's weight has increased and his mood has lifted. However, his secret exercising and ritualistic behaviour continues. Joe is unable to express his true feelings.

6. Groups

- Joe attends art therapy, family therapy and cognitive behavioural therapy and has one-to-one meetings with care team.

Education report

The education manager at the day unit reported next. Joe was settled in class but was bored. This was understandable, as there were very few group sessions due to the range of age and ability. It had been noted that Joe found difficulty in understanding written instructions for some subjects, but it was recognised that this might be due to his illness. Joe had expressed a wish to be reintegrated back into his class at his mainstream school before the end of the summer term.

Joe's form teacher from his mainstream school reported next. He had taught Joe for two years and so knew him well. He described Joe as an excellent sportsman who was very popular with his peers, but who did not have a similar rapport with adults. He stated that academically Joe had been in the top stream but struggled in some subjects. Joe had been in the same peer group for the past four years. He excelled in maths but was in the lower quartile of the class for other subjects. He produced some of Joe's work, showing how the style and presentation had changed as Joe became more and more ill. He showed some of Joe's more recent work which was back to normal. He admitted that Joe strives for perfection, which Dr Cornwall felt, was the root of his problem.

He wrapped up by saying he was very keen for Joe to be reintegrated into school before the end of term.

Discussion

Dr Cornwall informed the meeting that superficially Joe had moved on very quickly and that the team had reservations about him moving on so fast. I countered this by saying that I was worried about the impact on Joe if he was still in The Great Barn over the summer holidays. Joe's experience of the Easter holidays had not been a pleasant one as things were much more haphazard at the unit than in term time. Joe's stepfather added that they were very keen that Joe should be back in his own school by September.

Joe's case manager Fiona told the meeting that Joe fits into the textbook case of anorexia nervosa in that he is a perfectionist, obsessed with exercise and wants to be discharged as quickly as possible.

Dr Davis then spoke. He was the psychiatrist who had initially seen Joe as an out-patient and Joe would be referred back to him once he was discharged. He said he didn't think it was an unrealistic target to get Joe back into school by September. He felt the real issue to be discussed was his reintegration back into school this term.

I had pre-prepared a schedule showing what was happening at Joe's school between the date of this meeting and the end of term. There were six weeks left. The school exams finished in three weeks and so it seemed appropriate for Joe to start going back to school the week after the exams when things were more relaxed.

Finally medication was discussed. Joe's medical team continued to believe that Joe might benefit from taking an SSRI to suppress his obsessive tendencies. James, Joe and I were still not convinced that this was the right course of action for Joe. It was agreed that this should be delayed for a few more weeks to see if Joe could engage further with his cognitive behavioural sessions.

At the end of the meeting Joe was called in. He looked small and nervous as he entered this room full of adults. He came and sat down next to me and looked at Dr Cornwall in anticipation. She explained that they were all very pleased with Joe's progress, but that there was still some way to go. The good news was that Joe could start going back to school for a few days at a time in three weeks time. There could be no firm promises at this stage, but if school reintegration went well and Joe managed to maintain his weight and stay in a good mood, then they could consider his discharge later on in the summer.

Joe seemed to take all this on board but didn't seem terribly pleased. Dr

Cornwall asked Joe if he had any questions.

When can I come off the re-feeding table?'

This was a fair question. Joe had reached his target weight and was fed up to the back teeth of the endless hours of sitting at the re-feeding table with Phoebe. Fiona explained that they needed to make sure his weight had stabilised before he could make the move to the maintenance table. This was too much for Joe to take. He became tearful and I knew the floodgates were about to open. Once again he felt that all the promises made to him had been broken. The room emptied leaving me with Joe and James. For the next twenty minutes he howled and screamed and shouted and kicked the furniture in his frustration. I felt like crying too, but by this time I had learned that The Great Barn had very strict policies for children with eating disorders and it was no use trying to question them. Eventually Joe calmed down and then he managed to take on board the good news about being allowed back to school in a few weeks' time. He was definitely making progress and there was light at the end of the tunnel.

Recommendations following the professionals' meeting

- Medication to be delayed.

- Joe should re-integrate into school for the last three weeks of term, commencing 17th June for two days, 24th June for three days and 1st July for four days.

- Next professionals' meeting to be scheduled for 3rd July. If Joe's weight has stabilised and he is making good progress, then aim for his discharge around the middle of the summer holidays.

- Joe will be discharged to the care of Dr Davis, the community psychiatrist, and his team, which include family and cognitive behavioural therapists.

- Meanwhile the nursing team to consider level four observations at night for one week to assess Joe's activity levels.

Family therapy

The next day we had our second family therapy session. Tom was even less communicative than in the last session and spent the whole time drawing a cricket bat. He had just been in his first cricket match for the school and was still very excited about it. The therapist tried to involve Tom in the conversation on several occasions but his mind was clearly elsewhere. In contrast Joe was more talkative. We talked about the fact that until recently I had always worked full time and often travelled away on business. Joe said he had never known any different and hadn't minded having nannies and childminders. He knew I would always be there at the weekends. The therapist wondered how Joe had felt when I started working from home, about six months previously. Joe said it was good to have me around more but that he hated the fact that my work phone was always ringing. The therapist suggested that perhaps my being at home had put more pressure on Joe, if he was used to having a nanny. Joe said he didn't really know if that was the case. Joe said he was pleased that I was giving up work altogether because the phone wouldn't always be ringing. What was clear from this session was that we as a family would have to adjust to me being at home all the time and we would have to be careful to make sure that everyone was happy in this new family set-up.

The next session was scheduled for the end of June and would be a joint session with the therapist from the day centre and the family therapist from the community team. In that session we would plan to talk about reintegrating Joe back into family life after his discharge.

A family day out

That weekend we were all going to a cricket match. This was an annual event and we always went with another family who had children the same age as Joe and Tom. Once again we were given strict guidelines and a detailed menu plan. Sunday's menu plan was slightly different from usual as we would be having a picnic lunch at the cricket match and a meal in a pub before taking Joe back to The Great Barn. We had a lovely day out. Joe ate all his meals and was happy and relaxed all weekend.

Joe's ninth weekly review

Joe's weight had risen to 39.8 kg from 39.3 kg. Despite still being on the re-feeding table Joe had been allowed to prepare his own breakfast under staff supervision. Joe's care team were impressed that Joe had managed to pull himself together after the professionals' meeting and had settled back into daily life at The Great Barn. However, it was generally agreed that Joe was still angry with Fiona, his case manager, and perhaps in some way was blaming her for the fact that he was still in hospital.

There were two major decisions for Joe this week. The first was that he was allowed to move onto the maintenance table. The second was that all restrictions on exercise and activity were lifted. However, Joe was told in no uncertain terms that if his weight started to drop either through too much exercising, or not enough food intake, then he would be moved back onto the re-feeding table. Joe was understandably ecstatic. He enjoyed his first meal on the maintenance table and then as it was a lovely evening joined several of the other patients for a game of hide and seek in the garden. At last Joe felt he was getting back to normal.

More time at home

That weekend Joe came home from Friday afternoon to Tuesday evening. Because his re-feeding programme had finished we were no longer given guidance on his meals or snacks, but we had already been well prepared over the previous weekends.

On the Friday evening we went to a barbecue at the boys' school. It was an annual event, which both boys and parents looked forward to and everyone was pleased to see Joe looking so well. He devoured several sausages and a burger and then came back for cakes and other snacks, which were on offer. He had a fantastic evening playing all sorts of games with his friends. Thus far he had kept in contact with his closest friends and the cricket team. Now it was a joy to see him mixing happily with all and sundry.

We had a fairly quiet weekend although we were all up early on the Sunday to watch England play Sweden in the football World cup. On Sunday afternoon Joe made his first step towards taking responsibility for his food intake. When I called him in for his afternoon drink of milk he stated he would rather have some Lucozade Sport. I didn't want to have a big fight over a glass of milk, but I felt it was too early for Joe to be dropping his milk snack. Joe looked as if he was going to fly into a rage, but at the last minute decided he would have his milk. As he sat down at the table he muttered something under his breath, which I couldn't decipher, but at least he drank his milk.

On the Monday we went to a Jubilee street party in our old street. It was a long day and there was no escape for Joe when he got tired. We ended up coming home quite early as I could see Joe was flagging. He went to bed early and slept for hours.

Because it was the Jubilee, the Whitsun bank holiday fell on the Tuesday. We had a quiet day at home and Joe spent much of the time playing with Tom and his three stepsiblings. There was some gentle football in the garden and later all five children settled down in the living room to play monopoly. It was good to see Joe spending more time with his siblings but he was starting to look very tired. I hoped that the long weekend at home hadn't been too much for him. He went back to The Great Barn on the Tuesday evening without any complaint.

Joining in with the group activities

As it was school half term holiday the staff at The Great Barn had organised several trips out. As Joe was now on the maintenance table he was allowed to join in. On Wednesday Joe enjoyed a trip to the seaside and on Thursday a trip to a theme park. Suddenly life at The Great Barn wasn't quite so bad.

Joe's tenth weekly review meeting

Having had a week of being on a maintenance diet, having been allowed unrestricted exercise and having spent four days at home we were relieved to find out that Joe hadn't lost any weight. In fact his weight had crept up slightly from 39.8 kg to 40 kg.

Having had just two days back at The Great Barn, Joe came home again on the Friday morning. He came early that weekend. First it was my birthday and patients often went home for their parents' birthdays. Second, England were playing their second world cup match at lunchtime.

Once again we had an uneventful weekend. Joe enjoyed watching the football on TV, spent some time with his friends and some time just relaxing and enjoying being at home. Joe ate and drank everything I gave him without any resistance and seemed very happy. There were no signs of any obsessive or ritualistic behaviour. Joe knew he had just one more full week at The Great Barn before he would be starting his school reintegration.

Joe's eleventh weekly review meeting

After his second week on a maintenance diet Joe's weight increased from 40 kg to 40.6 kg. His weight was now above the top of his target range, but it was clear that he had grown over the last month and so his target weight range would have to be reassessed.

As Joe was continuing to do so well it was agreed that he could come home for one night mid-week to watch the next England game, as long as he was back at the day centre for education the next day.

The first signs of resistance

That weekend we noticed the first signs that Joe wanted to take responsibility for his own food intake. Up until that time he had been happy to follow our guidance at home and the care team's guidance at The Great Barn. It was a hot weekend and on Saturday, when I called Joe in for a glass of milk mid-morning he stated that he would much rather have a bottle of Lucozade Sport as it would be much better for quenching his thirst. I suggested that he could have both and Joe agreed, but I noticed he barely drank half the milk before tipping the rest down the sink. When I asked him why he had done this he told me not to fuss and was adamant that there had only been a tiny bit left in the glass. That afternoon he refused to have milk. He had some friends round and used them as an excuse. He said it made him look babyish having to have so much milk when all his friends were drinking soft drinks or water. I could see his point and so I agreed he could have Lucozade Sport instead as long as he had a larger glass of milk than normal at bedtime. This was an acceptable compromise for both of us and Joe dutifully had a large glass of milk later on. Apart from the milk issue he ate everything I put in front of him.

On the Sunday Joe decided it was time to push the boundaries further. We had a barbecue at lunchtime, of which he ate plenty. Then I dished up fruit salad with cream. Joe announced that he couldn't stand cream any more and he would rather have some low fat yoghurt. I had been buying cream in especially for Joe because it is not something we tend to have in our normal day-to-day life. Cream was really useful for topping up Joe's calories and I was adding plenty in cooking Joe's meals, which Joe didn't really notice. Given the flexibility that I had to squeeze in these extra calories elsewhere I agreed that Joe could have some yoghurt with his fruit. However, I reminded Joe in no uncertain terms that if he started to lose weight he would be likely to be back on the re-feeding table very quickly. Joe didn't like the sound of this and promised he would make up the calories elsewhere. Sure enough he ate several biscuits before I took him back to The Great Barn, as if to prove a point.

With regard to milk it was clear that Joe felt he had set a precedent the day before. He had a small glass of milk in the morning but refused to have any in the afternoon. I explained that I would have to report this back to his care team but Joe was in defiant mood. He claimed that now he was off the re-feeding table he didn't have to have his milk snacks any more.

Over the course of the next few weeks Joe continued to negotiate when the issue of eating dairy products arose. He claimed that he had been fed so much milk, cream and cheese at The Great Barn that he couldn't bear to eat them at home. Each time the issue came up I reminded Joe of the consequences if he lost weight. Each time he assured me that he would make up the calories elsewhere and he was happy to top up with biscuits and cakes. At the same time I added extra milk, cheese and cream to Joe's meals and I felt we had come to a satisfactory compromise. For the main part Joe accepted that he still had to eat more than everyone else to maintain his weight and we saw no signs of him seeking to restrict his diet in other areas.

School reintegration

That week Joe went back to school on Tuesday and Wednesday. I picked him up early Tuesday morning. The school exams had been held the previous week so I hoped that Joe would find the atmosphere reasonably relaxed. We had prepared carefully for Joe's return. Joe's form teacher, Mr Dunston had given me his timetable and we had chosen Joe's first few days carefully so there was a good balance of academic lessons and games. Mr Dunston had spoken to Joe's classmates about his return and it was agreed that two of his best friends would focus on helping Joe settle back in and would make sure he was occupied at breaktimes. We had agreed that for this week at least I would bring Joe home for lunch.

Both days went well and Joe clearly enjoyed being back in his old surroundings. He told me that most of the lessons were spent going over the exams and he was mightily relieved that he hadn't had to sit them. He thoroughly enjoyed athletics on the Tuesday afternoon and cricket on the Wednesday afternoon. Both sessions involved quite a lot of sitting around in the sun so Joe didn't over-stretch himself.

Joe's twelfth weekly review meeting

After his third week on the maintenance table and two days back at school, Joe's weight had slipped slightly from 40.6 kg to 40.2 kg. At The Great Barn, the care team had noticed that Joe was helping himself to the minimum portions of food that he could get away with and was choosing fruit rather than pudding. Joe also had to be reminded to have a drink with his main meal. On a couple of occasions when Joe had accepted drinks of water between meals he had been seen either tipping them away or over his head to cool himself down.

Very different views on progress

At this stage it was clear that Joe's care team had a very different view of Joe's recovery than the family had and it became evident that he was behaving in a different way when he was at The Great Barn compared to when he was at home. The care team felt that we were pushing Joe's recovery too quickly at home and that we were letting Joe push beyond the limits of his weekly review boundaries.

When Joe was at home, apart from avoiding dairy products, he was eating everything we gave him, he was in good humour, he wasn't displaying ritualistic tendencies and he was sleeping well. We may well have been looking through rose tinted glasses at this stage, but everything seemed to be going very well. Joe was above his target weight and looked in similar physical shape as his peers at school.

When Joe was at The Great Barn his care team observed a different scenario. It may be that they were simply better trained and knew what to look for. It may be that Joe was angry about still being there and this led to him being more anxious and rebellious. At this week's review meeting Joe's care team made the following comments:

1. Social Interaction

- Joe interacts with peers on the unit and school friends at the weekend. He is popular on the unit and is nurtured and fussed on by the other patients. They refer to Joe as being 'sweet', 'cute' etc. which Joe appears to like.

- Joe is sarcastic to certain staff especially his care team. He is often critical of his case manager using humour and banter. Case manager reciprocates the banter, which Joe seems to enjoy.

2. Family contact

- Family report that weekend leave goes really well, but care team feel mum is pushing review guidelines.

3. Behaviour

- Joe takes minimal deserts and fluids when he thinks staff are not watching. He has not been able to give any insights to staff about his problems.

4. Cognitive

- Joe is continually on the move and appears tired at times. He is generally settled but has not engaged with staff over his problems.

- Joe states that he has never had any big problems, but cannot explain what 'big problems' are. Joe says he has no problems or worries over attending his mainstream school. In fact he says his only problem is being at The Great Barn.

Despite these concerns Joe was allowed home for the weekend and in the following week attended school for three days. On Sunday evening when I took Joe back to The Great Barn he sobbed all the way in the car. He said he couldn't stand being there any more. He loved being back at home and at school and just wanted to be normal. I reassured Joe that it wouldn't be for too much longer and told him that I was really proud of how well he had coped thus far. We were all looking forward to having him home permanently but we just needed to be sure that his weight was stable. Joe was only back at The Great Barn for two days before returning home for school reintegration.

This time he stayed at school for lunch and was observed by staff to be eating well and socially interacting with a wide range of boys at the lunch table.

Fiona tried to engage with Joe over how he felt he was progressing. Joe was happy to talk but denied that he had any problems with food or drink. Fiona also challenged Joe about the rituals that he had been observed doing at The Great Barn, but Joe simply replied that he wasn't aware he was doing any rituals.

Family therapy

That week we attended our third family therapy session. This session had more structure than the previous ones. The family therapist from the community team attended as well and we all took to her straight away. In the session we talked about Joe coming home. Given that he had been coming home so much over the past few weeks we had already overcome some of the hurdles. We had come to a compromise over the issue of Joe's dislike of dairy products, but apart from that there had been no major issues. One of the therapists wondered if Joe might feel vulnerable once he had been fully discharged because he would no longer have the security of returning to the strict regime of the unit every week. Joe's response was blunt. He couldn't wait to get home. He didn't think the staff at The Great Barn could do any more for him.

The therapist then wondered if we, as parents, would feel vulnerable. We agreed that we would feel much more responsible for Joe's continued wellbeing once he was discharged. However, we had been well prepared by the team and we knew what to look out for. In addition we were very impressed by the community team of doctors and nurses that would be taking over Joe's care. If there were any problems or we were worried about relapse we knew exactly who to contact.

One of the therapists asked Tom how he felt about Joe coming home. He replied he was very pleased because it meant we could all get back to normal.

At the end of the session the therapist from the unit wished us good luck and the community therapist said she looked forward to seeing us again once Joe had been home for a few weeks, to see how we were getting on.

Joe's thirteenth weekly review meeting

It was a relief to find out that, despite Joe's care teams concerns over his attitude to food and drink, his weight had increased to 40.9 kg from 40.2 kg. Joe's care team felt that Joe was exercising too much and observed that he appeared tired on occasions. Apart from that little else came out of his review meeting and it was agreed that the following week Joe should attend four days at school. This would be the last four days of term.

That weekend flew past. On Saturday it was the school open day. On Sunday it was the World Cup final. Joe seemed very relaxed although a couple of times he broached the subject of his professionals' meeting which was scheduled for the following Wednesday morning. He was desperate to know what the outcome would be, but of course we didn't know and couldn't make any promises. Joe's care team had hinted at a discharge at some stage in the summer holidays but a lot still depended on Joe's weight and their assessment of his mood. I was feeling nervous because I knew Joe's care team still had reservations about how much progress Joe had really made, but I tried not to let it show.

Joe's second professionals' meeting

Steve had come back from New Zealand to attend the meeting. We dropped the boys off at school and picked up Mr Dunston. We arrived at the day centre in plenty of time and sat in awkward silence waiting for the meeting to start. We were all feeling nervous. The meeting started in the same way as the last one with Fiona reading out her professionals' report, which discussed Joe's progress since the last professionals' meeting:

1. Physical

- Joe's weight has stabilised around 40 kg, ranging from 39.8 kg to 40.9 kg since the last meeting. However, his weight has dropped 0.8 kg to 40.1 kg this week. His initial target weight was set at 38 kg to 40 kg.

- Joe has remained compliant with meals and snacks at The Great Barn, although he needs encouragement with fluids at times.

- Mum has reported that Joe has questioned having his milk snack and while at home has wanted to drink Lucozade rather than water. Care team have advised that Joe should not be drinking Lucozade continually as a substitute for other fluids.

- Joe appears to have grown taller and is to be measured again.

- Joe's physical observations are within normal limits in terms of blood pressure, pulse and temperature. A blood test was done recently.

- Joe appears to sleep at night. He gets up at least once for the toilet. He still wakes and gets up early.

- Objectively staff report that Joe looks and appears tired, although he does not complain of feeling fatigued.

2. Hygiene

- Joe self-cares to a fair standard and appears to be cleaning himself, washing and showering on a regular basis. Joe's bedroom is a mess and he has not been seen changing his bed linen. Joe suggests this is not his job.

3. Social interactions

- Joe is popular with his peers and is liked by staff, interacting with them and enjoying any banter. Joe's humour is often sarcastic and although it is amusing, it could be suggested that his humour is used to avoid him being reprimanded for comments that can border on the offensive.

4. Family

- The family has kept in very close contact with Joe throughout the duration of his stay at The Great Barn. Joe's mother and stepfather have visited regularly. Since Joe's father returned to New Zealand he has kept in close contact with Joe, Joe's mother and the care team by phone. Both biological parents and family appear ready to do whatever is necessary in order to make Joe well. However, it is suggested that in such difficult emotional circumstances, ongoing guidance from the multi-disciplinary professionals' team is essential.

- Joe has put a huge amount of pressure on his mother to get him out of The Great Barn. Joe's mother has been very influential and prescriptive in steering Joe's care and has produced mapped out programmes in reference to Joe's home leave and school reintegration. The pace of care has been uncomfortable for the staff and Joe has not engaged in the nurse-patient relationship. Therefore there is serious concern that Joe's coping mechanisms when anxious will continue to be maladaptive. Having said this, the community team will continue to closely monitor Joe's progress and offer support.

5. Mood

- Joe appears bright, witty and interacts well. He prefers to socialise with his peers rather than staff. Joe appears settled when on the unit, but often appears tired.

6. Thoughts

- To start with Joe voiced school as a big problem. More recently in the community meeting he has claimed the only big problem he has is being at The Great Barn. When asked he has been unable to identify what he means by a 'big problem'.

7. Behaviour

- It appears to the care team that Joe has literally followed instructions in terms of putting weight on and getting out of The Great Barn.

- Most of the time Joe is active. Staff have observed Joe casually doing strenuous exercises such as using his arms to support his body weight in the frame of the doorway. There are still some ritualistic behaviours such as odd postures or movements.

- Joe has recently been trying to push the boundaries at home in terms of snacks and chooses to drink lots of Lucozade rather than other fluids. Joe's mother has asked him not to continually drink Lucozade but has suggested that this is probably Joe's way of 'getting his own way'.

- Joe avoids sitting with his care team for one-to-one work. Joe has spent very little time on the unit in the last few weeks, which has made it impossible to try and maintain any real alliance with him.

Discussion

It was clear that Fiona didn't think Joe was ready for discharge and that she believed there to be a high risk of relapse. In addition the fact that he had lost 0.8 kg in the past week was disappointing and slightly alarming. I felt torn. I knew how much Joe wanted to be discharged, but I didn't want this to happen if everyone else believed it was still too early.

In the event there ensued a very interesting debate. Everyone agreed that Joe had not engaged with the therapists at The Great Barn, but this didn't necessarily mean he wasn't ready for discharge.

The head of education at the day centre reported that Joe was enjoying his reintegration back into school. This isn't always the case and for some patients can be a major stumbling block on the road to recovery. Mr Dunston reported that there were no issues with school, even with his eating and felt that Joe had very easily fitted back in with his peers.

Dr Cornwall, Joe's consultant psychiatrist at The Great Barn stated that as Joe had already disengaged with The Great Barn team there was little point him staying any longer. Joe should continue to be weighed at his GP's surgery and should be transferred to the care of the community team. Joe's target weight range was currently 38 kg to 40 kg, but as Joe had grown it needed to be raised. It was felt that a 4 kg range would be appropriate, especially as Joe's weight was likely to fluctuate for a while as we worked out how much he needed to eat. It was clear that Joe would need to gain some weight to achieve the middle of his new range. I indicated that I was happy that I could manage Joe's diet to ensure he carried on gaining weight for a little while. I said that the menu plans that I had been given when Joe first came home at the weekends had been invaluable in teaching me how to create meals, which were easy to eat, yet contained enough calories.

Dr Davis, Joe's community consultant psychiatrist stated that he had a cognitive behavioural therapist and a family therapist on his team who could take over Joe's care on an out-patient basis. He reminded us that the most important factors to watch were Joe's weight and his mood. If either started to deteriorate alarm bells should start ringing. We needed to be constant about his weight level and if it dropped by more than a kg he would have to be readmitted.

It was agreed that Joe should be discharged immediately into the care of the community team. We arranged that Joe would return the following Tuesday to see Dr Cornwall and to have a goodbye party at The Great Barn.

After the meeting I reflected that recovering from anorexia was a bit like learning to drive. Joe had done everything he needed to do to pass his test and to be let out on his own. In the next few months he would face many new challenges and would have to learn to cope with difficult situations that he hadn't faced whilst in the security of The Great Barn. We would support him as best we could. It felt as if we had been preparing for this day for a long time. Now we, as a family, were about to face the real test. Could we prevent Rex from rearing his ugly head in our house again?

19. Coming home – will Rex come too?

After the professionals' meeting we went back to The Great Barn to pick up Joe's things. Given that he had been spending so much time at home recently there wasn't an awful lot left in his room, but it still felt strange when we shut the door on the empty room that would soon be occupied by another young person. Joe had been through a huge amount of emotional trauma in that room. It was a cheerful, bright corner room but I hoped he would never have to return to it.

By the time we got back home it was nearly lunchtime and so we drove to Joe's school to tell Joe the good news in his lunch break. He looked very worried when we met up with him at the school. He had clearly been agonising all morning about the outcome of the professionals' meeting. He had been so disillusioned after the first professionals' meeting when he felt he was making no progress. When we told him he had been discharged his face lit up. He couldn't quite believe it and kept asking if he would have to go back for sessions at the day centre or group therapy at The Great Barn, or for any other reason. We gave him the normal health warning that he would have to maintain a healthy weight, but as long as he managed this he was definitely home for good. All he had to do was return one more time to see Dr Cornwall, his consultant psychiatrist, and to attend his leaving party with the other patients.

As it was near the end of term, there were house cricket matches going on all afternoon and we left a very happy boy, determined to play well for his house team, and looking forward to returning to a normal life.

A successful weekend trip

That weekend Steve took Joe and Tom for a three-day trip to Thorpe Park. As he hadn't been involved in Joe's day-to-day eating requirements since he had been coming home, I gave Steve a sheet with guidance on how much food Joe needed to eat to maintain his weight. Steve didn't think it would be a problem to fill Joe up with burgers, ice cream and large hotel meals, but we all knew how difficult Joe had been in the past and so Steve promised to make sure that Joe didn't use the trip as an excuse to cut down on food. Joe's care team at The Great Barn had made it very clear to us that they felt there was a high risk of relapse. It is one thing establishing a healthy eating regime at home. It is an entirely different issue when you move away from a routine. I knew from all the reading I had done, that holidays could be very difficult times for recovering anorexics. They still feel uncertain how much they should be eating and the abundance of rich and fattening foods can frighten them. As it turned out both Joe and Tom had a lovely break with their dad and both returned on the Tuesday morning looking tanned and healthy.

A sobering discharge meeting and a goodbye party

I took Joe back to the day centre that afternoon. He wasn't looking forward to his meeting with Dr Cornwall but he was looking forward to his leaving party. He had become firm friends with several of the other patients and was keen to say a proper goodbye.

Joe's meeting with Dr Cornwall was fairly sobering. She explained to Joe the importance of maintaining the appropriate weight for his age and height. She reiterated that Joe had done extremely well to maintain his weight within his target of 38 to 40 kg, but cautioned that he needed to be very careful especially given that his weight had fallen by 0.8 kg in the week before discharge to 40.1 kg. She then explained that the dietician had calculated a new target range for Joe because he had grown so much in the past three months. His new range was 40 to 44 kg. She told Joe that he would be weighed weekly at his GP's surgery and that if he could not retain his target weight he would have to return to The Great Barn for re-feeding at the weekends. If his weight dropped dramatically at any stage then of course he would be readmitted during the week as well.

Dr Cornwall's discharge report to Dr Davis was also fairly sobering. It cautioned that Joe had regained weight fairly rapidly, but he had not really engaged in his therapy and so had made far less progress cognitively. Joe had made some progress with cognitive behavioural therapy, but had found the CB strategies difficult to adopt. Joe continually denied he had any problems apart from being at The Great Barn. The care team had also commented that Joe still displayed ritualistic behaviour. Dr Cornwall also noted that the family had strongly resisted medication for Joe. Some patients with obsessive tendencies respond well to drug therapy, but we had not wanted Joe to be given drug therapy unless it was a last resort.

In contrast Joe had a fantastic leaving party. He said goodbye to all his friends and all his favourite members of staff were present. He came home armed with good luck notes and a beaming smile on his face. The next day he wrote to Fiona and several other members of the care team thanking them for putting up with him and for saving his life. He really did seem to appreciate how close he was to dying when he was first admitted to The Great Barn. He kept in touch with several of the other patients by phone and in writing over the course of the summer holidays although this petered out when he went back to school in September.

The next day Joe had several of his school friends round for a sleepover. It was so comforting to see him back with his old friends, playing football in the garden, larking about on the trampoline, playing computer games and watching TV. Joe wasn't at all nervous about eating in front of his friends and in fact happily ate more than they did. We had noticed over the past few weeks with Joe being at home more often, that he had to eat huge quantities just to maintain his weight. To gain weight he needed to add several extra high calorie snacks a day. Joe was still reluctant to have too much milk, cream and cheese, but made up for it by consuming huge amounts of everything else. It was still early days, but the initial signs were promising.

Endless appointments

The initial euphoria of being at home soon wore off when, later that week Joe had to face up to the realities of being an out-patient. He might have escaped from The Great Barn, but he certainly hadn't escaped from the doctors. Our GP's surgery had agreed that one of their doctors would weigh Joe every Thursday morning as close to 9 am as possible. We had to ensure that Joe wore similar clothes each week, and of course watch out for any signs that he was artificially boosting his weight by drinking excessively pre-weighing or by hiding heavy objects in his clothes. In fact Joe never did this, but it is a very common trick that recovering anorexics play. Joe was seen by a young male doctor who we hadn't met before. He soon put Joe at his ease by asking if Joe had been following the world cup finals. He explained to Joe that he would be weighing him once a week and that he understood that Joe's target weight range was 40 to 44 kg. Joe stepped on the scales and weighed 39.5 kg. My heart sank and Joe turned pale, but the doctor seemed fairly relaxed. He said he knew that Joe's target range had just been increased and that ideally Joe's weight should be nearer the middle of the range. However, given that Joe had had a very busy week since being discharged, and taking into account that the doctor's scales might show a slightly different weight to those at The Great Barn, there wasn't too much cause for concern. He reiterated that Joe needed to gain some weight and hoped that Joe would be able to gain a little by the following Thursday. Joe seemed to really like this doctor and promised that he would make an extra effort to gain some more weight.

On Friday we had an appointment with Dr Davis, Joe's consultant psychiatrist at the Child and Family Mental Health Service. He was very pleased to see that Joe had been eating well, sleeping well and was generally in good spirits. He asked about Joe's attitude to exercise and was pleased to hear that Joe was doing lots of social exercise with his peers but was showing no signs of trying to do repetitive exercise alone. However, he reiterated the message that Joe had been given by the young doctor the day before. Joe really needed to try to maintain his weight near to the middle of his target range. He suggested to Joe that he try to eat a few more snacks in between meals, which would help increase his overall calorie intake.

The following Tuesday Joe had his first appointment with the cognitive behavioural therapist at the Child and Family Mental Health Service. She was very different to the CB therapist that Joe had seen at The Great Barn and Joe was in no mood to open up to her. She explained that they would be meeting on a weekly basis and would try to continue to develop some of the CB strategies that Joe had already been introduced to at The Great Barn. On the way home Joe was in defiant mood. He stated that he was better so why should he carry on seeing all these doctors. He felt it was going to ruin his summer holidays. I reminded him how much better it was to be at home and having to go to several appointments a week rather than being at The Great Barn all the time. Joe accepted this but was still unhappy. "Mummy, I just want to be back to normal like all my friends!"

Two days later we were back at the GP's surgery for Joe's weekly weighing session. Joe weighed 40 kg and the doctor praised Joe's efforts to eat more and encouraged him to keep up the good work.

The following Tuesday Joe had his second session with his CB therapist. He talked more openly in this session about losing weight and wanting to be better at sport. He spoke at length about how he felt, as he became weaker and weaker until he could no longer do any sport. He told her that he had wanted to get better so he could do sport again but once he arrived at The Great Barn he just wanted to be back home again. He hadn't realised how long he would have to stay at The Great Barn and he certainly didn't ever want to go back. The CB therapist noted that Joe became tearful when talking about his illness, but when she asked him why he was tearful he couldn't explain. At the end of the session she told Joe that now that they had got to know each other better they could begin some thought work at the next session. Joe had started to do this with the CB therapist at The Great Barn and so knew that this work would involve identifying negative thoughts and then trying to challenge them.

At the GP's surgery on Thursday Joe weighed 40.5 kg. He was making steady progress in gaining weight and the doctor was very pleased with him.

The next day Joe had a lengthy orthodontist appointment, which took up half the day as it was at a hospital an hour's drive from home. Joe was utterly fed up with seeing doctors by this stage and felt it was interfering with his social life. In the three weeks he had been at home he had attended seven appointments. In general Joe was very happy, eating well, gaining weight and sleeping well. The one thing that made him unhappy was the endless doctor's appointments. I sympathised but felt very strongly that he should continue to attend these appointments. Joe had been extremely ill and the risk of relapse was still high. So despite his regular protestations I insisted that Joe carry on seeing the doctors and having his therapy sessions.

The worst week for Joe was the week beginning the 5th August:

- On Monday he had a CB session, which Joe found difficult because he didn't want to address the negative thoughts he had had about food and weight when he was ill. He just wanted to put his illness behind him and be normal like all his friends. The CB therapist had some success in getting Joe to identify situations he still found difficult. The main one he identified was that he felt that all his friend's mums were constantly trying to get him to eat. This was partly my fault as I had explained to his friend's mums that Joe needed to eat lots of snacks in order to gain a little more weight. Joe felt that I should have been able to trust him to use his own judgement on this when he was at a friend's house.

- On Tuesday we all attended family therapy. The therapist was very different to the one we had had at The Great Barn and we all found it easier to talk to her. However, this might have been because we were all more relaxed now that Joe was at home and doing so well. Joe looked very relieved when she said we seemed to be coping so well that she didn't feel we needed to see her again. Of course we were welcome to book an appointment if we felt one was needed at any time in the future.

- On Thursday Joe was weighed at the GP's surgery. His weight had stabilised at 41 kg and the doctor advised Joe that he needed to try to gain a little more weight.

- On Friday I took Joe to see Dr Davis, his consultant psychiatrist. Dr Davis was very pleased with Joe's weight gain and encouraged him to carry on the good work. Joe talked happily about how much he was enjoying being back at home and that he didn't have any fears about food anymore. He realised he had to eat more than his friends to maintain a reasonable weight and that extra snacks could help him to gain a little more weight. However, when Dr Davis brought up the subject of continuing therapy Joe became very tearful and angry. Joe said again that he wanted to put his illness behind him, but all the time he was having therapy he couldn't do this. Dr Davis explained that the purpose of ongoing therapy was to help Joe to change his thought processes so that he could cope better with difficult situations in his life in the future. He explained that relapse rates were high in anorexia and if Joe didn't address his thought processes he could be vulnerable to a relapse in the future. Joe was not going to be persuaded and was very sullen throughout the meeting. However, Dr Davis and I both agreed that Joe should continue his therapy sessions for the time being.

The following week Joe only had one appointment as his CB therapist was on holiday. This fitted in well because Joe was attending a five-day football course with some of his friends and he would have been very upset if he had had to keep going off for various appointments. Joe really enjoyed being back on the football field. He trained and played hard, but consumed enough food and drink to maintain his weight at 41 kg.

For the last two weeks of the summer holidays we went on a family holiday in France. There were twelve of us altogether staying in two separate caravans. Joe's cousin is also a keen footballer and the two boys attended a football course every morning. It was a very well run course with lots of fitness and skills training. Joe was certainly going to be in good shape for the start of the football season when he went back to school. I was slightly worried that Joe would find it difficult to eat enough in the slightly hotter climate, but my worries were unfounded. Joe maintained his weight and topped up his tan. He looked the picture of health when we returned home at the end of August.

Joe and Tom both went back to school in good spirits. I had already had several meetings with Joe's new form teacher so she fully understood what he had been through and that there was still a risk of relapse. This was a critical time for Joe. He had coped extremely well with the transition from The Great Barn to home life, but being back at school full time was a very different scenario. How would Joe cope in his new class? How would Joe cope with being a full time pupil again with a demanding academic timetable? How would Joe cope if he wasn't made football captain? How would Joe cope if anyone commented on his new physique or teased him about his illness? There were lots of unknowns and I wanted to make sure Joe was given as much support as possible.

The first week was very relaxed. The boys were given their timetable and introduced to the new teachers. Books were handed out and brought home to be covered. Apart from that there seemed to be very little work and quite a lot of sport. Traditionally the school had a house football competition in the first week. This gave all the boys that wanted to a chance to play in a team. It also gave the sports-masters a chance to pick boys for the school teams.

Joe's house team did very well and by Friday had got in to the final. Parents were invited along to watch the final and I went along feeling both excited and nervous. Joe's team went two nil down in the first half. Joe looked forlorn but didn't give up. In the second half Joe's team scored early on in a goalmouth scramble. Both sides had several chances after that, but failed to put the ball in the back of the net. Then in the last minute Joe made a fantastic run down the right wing. He passed the ball into the centre, but it was cleared by a defender. Joe intercepted the clearance, sidestepped the defender and fired the ball into the back of the net. The match was a draw and would go to a penalty shoot out. I could hardly watch. Joe took the first penalty, was cool as a cucumber and put the ball firmly in the back of the net. The next nine penalties were also taken successfully so it was sudden death. Joe stepped up to take the first penalty. He looked a little more nervous this time and didn't strike the ball quite so well, but the goalkeeper went the wrong way. Joe had scored. The opposition failed to score their next penalty so Joe's team had won. Joe and his team were ecstatic. It was the first time their house had won the house competition for five years. When they had all calmed down the head of sports made a presentation. He also chose this opportunity to confirm that Joe would be the captain of the U13 first team for football. I hadn't seen Joe look so happy for a long time. All of his friends rallied round to congratulate him. He was obviously a popular choice amongst the boys.

After the euphoria of the first week back at school Joe found the second week much harder. There was a lot of homework on topics that Joe hadn't covered in much depth before. He scored badly a couple of times and was asked to repeat the work. James and I gave him as much help and support as we could and he managed to avoid getting a detention for poor work. Joe also found a full week at school very tiring and found it difficult to concentrate all day. I went to see Joe's form teacher to make sure she understood that it might take Joe a little while to settle back in to full time school life. She was very sympathetic and assured us that Joe was not alone. Lots of the boys found it difficult to settle after the long summer holidays. She was very pleased to report that socially Joe seemed to be doing very well and he had been observed to be eating huge platefuls of food at lunchtime. In fact by the end of the second week Joe's weight had risen to 42 kg. Thus far there were no signs of Joe's anorexia re-emerging.

20. Moving on – Rex has gone!

By the end of September Joe had fully settled back into school. We had a meeting with Joe's key teachers and they agreed that his transition back into school life was going extremely well. He was much happier in his new class and was coping well with all the academic subjects, although there were clearly a few gaps in his knowledge from his period of absence. His teachers were all very relaxed about this and didn't think it would take too much time for him to catch up. Socially he had fitted back into his year group with ease, both with his old buddies and with his new classmates. The teachers all felt that Joe had regained his sense of humour and got his sparkle back. Joe's sports teacher commented on his fitness and thought that he was going to be an excellent football captain. He had also noticed that Joe was taking some of the younger boys in the team squad under his wing, making sure that they didn't feel out of depth suddenly playing with the bigger, older boys. With regard to school dinners and breaks, Joe had returned to being a normal teenage boy with a huge appetite, which was a good thing given all the sport he was doing. We all agreed that Joe should continue to be weighed once a week by the school nurse and I pointed out that Joe still had to have regular appointments with his psychiatrist and his cognitive behavioural therapist. Apart from that he should be able to continue leading a perfectly normal school life.

These regular appointments continued to be a bone of contention with Joe. He knew his weight was fine, he felt happy both at home and at school. Why did he have to keep seeing the doctors? When I explained to him about the possibility of relapse he felt I didn't trust him and I could understand why he felt that way. In the end we reached a compromise. I promised to discuss the whole issue of therapy with Joe's consultant at our next meeting which was scheduled for a month's time, if Joe agreed to continue seeing the cognitive behavioural therapist on a weekly basis at least until that time. Joe accepted this but still became tearful the next time we drove to his CB appointment. He explained to me that the therapy sessions just reminded him of how ill he had been and he simply wanted to put it all behind him.

Two weeks later Joe went on a school French trip to Le Touquet. He would be away for three nights and there was a very busy itinerary. He was very excited about the prospect of three nights away with his friends. I have to admit that I was very nervous. It would be the first time he had been away from home on his own since his illness. When he got on the coach early on the Monday morning I felt like a young mother dropping her son off at school for the first time. I could feel the tears welling up as the coach drove away, despite the fact that I could see Joe sat on the back seat happily chatting with all his pals. Of course he had a fantastic time, although several boys in the group had been afflicted by a nasty stomach bug. He also said that the food had been a bit odd and not really to his liking but he seemed in good health and good spirits so there seemed little cause for concern.

Unfortunately, the stomach bug came home with the boys and by the end of the week most of the boys in Joe's class, including Joe, had been struck down. Joe was very poorly for a few days and could hardly drink a glass of water let alone eat a proper meal. Even when he was over the worst his appetite continued to be poor. I tried talking to Joe about the importance of maintaining his weight. He promised me that he understood this and he wasn't trying to lose weight, he just didn't feel like eating much because he wasn't doing so much sport. Alarm bells were ringing in my head but I tried not to panic. We were just about to go on holiday to the Caribbean for a week and I didn't want to spoil the holiday by nagging at Joe about his weight.

The Caribbean sunshine was a reviving tonic for the whole family. It had been a tough year and we had all been looking forward to a relaxing and warm seaside holiday. Joe and Tom both made friends as soon as we arrived at the resort and after that we saw them in the distance sailing, playing tennis, playing beach volleyball, swimming and generally having a lovely time. The boys often ate their meals with their friends so it was difficult to judge how much Joe was eating, but he was obviously having a lovely time so I started to relax again. It was a very active holiday and we all came back feeling fitter and healthier than we had for a long time.

The following Monday Joe had a CB session which, for once, he seemed very relaxed about. The next day I took Joe back to see his psychiatrist Dr Davis. Sure enough his weight had dropped to just over 40 kg. I was expecting words of caution but Dr Davis was unfazed by Joe's weight. He felt that the combination of a foreign school trip, a nasty bug and a foreign holiday would all have contributed to this loss of weight. He and Joe's CB therapist both felt that Joe was in very good spirits and appeared to be much more relaxed talking about food and weight. I agreed that eating didn't seem to be an issue for Joe anymore, but pointed out that I still felt nervous if Joe didn't eat for any reason. Dr Davis reassured me that this was a perfectly normal reaction from a mother who had watched her son become so ill. As I had promised I also spoke to Dr Davis about Joe continuing weekly CB therapy. Given how well Joe was doing mentally Dr Davis felt that it was appropriate to reduce the sessions to once a month. Dr Davis then had a talk with Joe on his own in which he praised Joe for doing so well, but reiterated that it was very important for Joe to keep within his target weight range. Joe's weight was right at the bottom of the range at the moment so he should make every effort to try to gain a little weight. Once again Dr Davis reminded Joe that the more sport he did, the more he needed to eat. Joe accepted these words of advice happily and we both left in good spirits.

Joe continued to do well at school for the remainder of the term. Despite playing football at every opportunity, Joe managed to gradually gain weight and by the end of term weighed 43 kg. The football team had a very successful term and Joe was awarded the football skills prize at the end of term. At home he was happy and relaxed. Food was no longer an issue and

Joe gradually started consuming more dairy products of his own accord. For example, he was happy to have an ice cream at the cinema, to eat a pizza with his friends and to take a glass of milk up to bed. He had a CB session at the beginning of December, which he attended happily.

We had a wonderfully relaxed Christmas at home. It was the first time for years that the Joe and Tom had spent Christmas at home because previously they had always travelled abroad to see their father. It also meant that Joe spent his thirteenth birthday at home. It was the first time I had seen him on his birthday since he was three. Joe's father had recently moved back to the UK so the boys saw lots of him over the Christmas holidays, but they also had plenty of time to relax at home and see their friends.

Joe went back to school in January in much happier spirits than he had the year before. At the end of January I took Joe back to see Dr Davis. He was delighted to see how well Joe looked and that his weight had increased to 44 kg. Both his height and weight were just above the 50th centile for his age on the boy's growth charts. Joe saw the CB therapist whilst I talked to Dr Davis. He asked if I had any concerns at all about either Joe's physical or mental condition. I answered that I was extremely happy with Joe's progress, but I just wanted to let Dr Davis know that Joe still had a few funny habits left over from his anorexic days. He still picked up rubbish, he still hesitated when stepping from one room to another and he still touched walls. Dr Davis asked if these habits had any negative implications either for Joe or others in the family. As they didn't he advised me to ignore them and they would probably disappear in due course. I also mentioned that Joe still had some periods of moderately low self-esteem, but they were becoming more and more infrequent. Again Dr Davis felt this was a minor hangover from the anorexia which would clear in time. Dr Davis reiterated to me that he felt Joe and the family had come along way in six months. Anorexia is a very difficult disease to beat but we seemed to have all pulled together and done a good job. He felt comfortable in discharging Joe from his care. Of course, if we were at all concerned in the future we could get a referral back to Dr Davis from our GP. However Dr Davis felt that Joe's prognosis was very good and didn't envisage that we would have to go down this route.

Joe and the CB therapist then joined us. Dr Davis told Joe how pleased he was with his progress and that Joe should be very proud of his success in beating his illness. Joe was delighted that he was being discharged and said that with no more therapy sessions he would feel like a completely normal boy again. He thanked Dr Davis and the CB therapist for the time they had spent with him and although he didn't actually say, "I hope I never see you both again," you could see that that was exactly what he was thinking.

From that day on we have never looked back. In March Joe won the annual school cross-country race, which he had so desperately wanted to win the previous year, but had been too ill to participate in. In the summer term Joe represented the school at cricket and athletics and did very well in his end of year exams. At prize giving he was awarded the football prize (which we already knew about) the athletics prize, the maths prize and the geography prize. We were all very proud of him, not just because he had had such a successful year at school, but also because he had successfully put his anorexia well and truly behind him.

In December 2003 a baby sister joined Joe's chaotic family. Joe and all his other siblings adore her.

The final episode was the writing of this book. As Joe said, "If one other family benefits from reading this book it will have been well worthwhile."

CPSIA information can be obtained at www.ICGtesting.com
Printed in the USA
LVOW09*1500161214

419116LV00014B/253/P